Plautus: *Casina*

BLOOMSBURY ANCIENT COMEDY COMPANIONS

Series editors: C. W. Marshall & Niall W. Slater

The Bloomsbury Ancient Comedy Companions present accessible introductions to the surviving comedies from Greece and Rome. Each volume provides an overview of the play's themes, and situates it in its historical and literary contexts, recognizing that each play was intended in the first instance for performance. Volumes will be helpful for students and scholars, providing an overview of previous scholarship and offering new interpretations of ancient comedy.

Aristophanes: Peace, Ian C. Storey
Plautus: Casina, David Christenson
Terence: Andria, Sander M. Goldberg

Plautus: *Casina*

David Christenson

BLOOMSBURY ACADEMIC
LONDON • NEW YORK • OXFORD • NEW DELHI • SYDNEY

BLOOMSBURY ACADEMIC
Bloomsbury Publishing Plc
50 Bedford Square, London, WC1B 3DP, UK
1385 Broadway, New York, NY 10018, USA

BLOOMSBURY, BLOOMSBURY ACADEMIC and the Diana logo are
trademarks of Bloomsbury Publishing Plc

First published in Great Britain 2019

Cover design: Terry Woodley
Cover image © DEA PICTURE LIBRARY / Getty

A catalogue record for this book is available from the British Library.

A catalog record for this book is available from the Library of Congress.

ISBN: HB: 978-1-3500-2054-2
         PB: 978-1-3500-2053-5
       ePDF: 978-1-3500-2056-6
      eBook: 978-1-3500-2055-9

Series: Bloomsbury Ancient Comedy Companions

Typeset by RefineCatch Limited, Bungay, Suffolk

To find out more about our authors and books visit www.bloomsbury.com
and sign up for our newsletters.

To students, the best teachers

Contents

Titles and Abbreviations:
Plautus's Plays

LATIN TITLE	ENGLISH TRANSLATION	ABBREVIATION
Amphitruo	*Amphitryon*	*Am.*
Asinaria	*The Comedy of Asses*	*As.*
Aulularia	*The Pot of Gold*	*Aul.*
Bacchides	*The Two Bacchises*	*Bac.*
Captiui	*The Captives*	*Capt.*
Casina	*Casina*	*Cas.*
Cistellaria	*The Casket Comedy*	*Cist.*
Curculio	*Curculio*	*Cur.*
Epidicus	*Epidicus*	*Epid.*
Menaechmi	*Menaechmi*	*Men.*
Mercator	*The Merchant*	*Mer.*
Miles Gloriosus	*The Braggart Soldier*	*Mil.*
Mostellaria	*The Haunted House*	*Mos.*
Persa	*The Persian*	*Per.*
Poenulus	*The Little Carthaginian*	*Poen.*
Pseudolus	*Pseudolus*	*Ps.*
Rudens	*The Rope*	*Rud.*

Stichus	*Stichus*	*St.*
Trinummus	*Three-Dollar Day*	*Trin.*
Truculentus	*Truculentus*	*Truc.*
Vidularia	*The Traveling-Bag Tale*	*Vid.*

Acknowledgements

This volume is one of three that launch the Bloomsbury Ancient Comedy Companions series. This exciting new series is designed to be accessible to non-specialists who do not know Greek or Latin but wish to engage critically with ancient comedies and scholarly debates about them. This study of Plautus's *Casina* reflects a conviction that these plays must first be understood and analysed as performances: the third chapter ('*Casina* in Performance') accordingly is this book's most detailed and extensive. While this volume primarily serves the needs of general readers, it is my hope that specialists in Plautine comedy will find some new interpretative points of interest to them here as well.

I owe special thanks to Alice Wright, Senior Commissioning Editor at Bloomsbury, for her guidance, encouragement and extraordinary patience throughout the entire production process. Editorial Assistant Emma Payne was instrumental in providing detailed and clear assistance in preparing the typescript, and Ronnie Hanna did an indispensable job of copy-editing. Series editors Toph Marshall and Niall Slater heroically scrutinized drafts during their theatrical tour of Greece, even finding time and energy to meticulously comment on these on buses to Meteora, Galaxadi and elsewhere. Their fine insights, critical acumen, and eyes and ears for good writing improved this book enormously (though they also allowed me freedom to indulge my own judgement, for better or worse).

Finally, I have dedicated this book to the students, both undergraduate and graduate, whose fresh takes on ancient literature constantly reinvigorate for me texts such as *Casina*. They remind me that the true business of the university is still the exchange of ideas.

Introduction to Plautine Comedy

Plot summary of *Casina*

A husband (Lysidamus) and wife (Cleostrata) seek a marriage for a sixteen-year-old slave (Casina, who does not appear in the play) that Cleostrata raised like a daughter after finding her as an exposed infant. Lysidamus wants Casina to marry his farm-manager (Olympio), so that he can sexually exploit her. Cleostrata, who knows that her son Euthynicus (he also is absent in the play) desires Casina, seeks to marry her to Euthynicus's military assistant (Chalinus), in order to frustrate her husband and help her son. Cleostrata and Lysidamus fail to dissuade each other's proxies from pursuing marriage with Casina and agree to leave the matter to chance in a drawing of lots. Olympio wins the lottery and Lysidamus makes plans to sexually assault Casina at the neighbouring house of his friend Alcesimus, who is married to Myrrhina, Cleostrata's close confidante. Chalinus overhears Lysidamus's plans and reports them to Cleostrata, who launches a scheme against her husband. This scheme is in full swing when Pardalisca (Cleostrata's slave/maid) delivers a fictional report to Lysidamus that an angry Casina wields two swords and is threatening to kill the old man and his farm-manager. Cleostrata, Myrrhina and Pardalisca engineer a play-within-the-play, in which Chalinus, dressed as the bride Casina, is married to Olympio. Olympio and Lysidamus are violently rebuffed by Chalinus during their 'honeymoon' inside Alcesimus's house. Brought back onstage, both master and slave are shamed by the female characters, and Lysidamus is forced to apologize to Cleostrata. In the epilogue we learn that Casina is the free-born daughter of Myrrhina and Alcesimus and will marry Euthynicus.[1]

'Old situations, / New complications, / Nothing portentous or polite; / Tragedy tomorrow, / Comedy tonight!' So runs a section of the opening song of the 1960s musical *A Funny Thing Happened on the Way to the Forum*, a lively pastiche of Plautine comedies including *Casina* that enjoyed great success on the stage and in its film version (see pp. 118–19). Just as Plautus served Roman theatregoers fresh treatments of the Greek comedies he was adapting over two millennia earlier, the modern musical, one more in a long line of Plautine spin-offs, promises its audience something new and funny. Who was this Latin playwright whose comedies continue to delight audiences?

Plautus the Latin comic playwright

The implausible-sounding moniker Titus Maccius Plautus – 'Dick, son of Clown, the Mime-actor' – is considered to be a pseudonym, not the name the future comic playwright we know as Plautus received at birth.[2] There is some evidence that the Roman first name Titus was the equivalent of 'Dick' in slang, and that Roman mime actors wore phalluses.[3] Moreover, mime actors were nicknamed 'flat-foots' because they performed barefoot, and *plautus* in Latin means 'flat'. The *Casina* prologue speaker's joke about Plautus's 'barking name' (34)[4] plays on the description of dogs with flat, floppy ears as *plauti*.[5] The stock clown of an Italian form of drama known as Atellan farce was named Maccus.[6] All this points to 'Plautus' being as much a biographical construction as the actual name of an historical playwright. At most, we can hypothesize from Plautus's name that he had experience in native Italian theatrical performances apart from his surviving work in the genre of Roman comedy based on Greek models.[7] Plautus is the first Roman playwright we know of to specialize in this latter comic genre. We know nothing about Plautus's social status, although the apparent fictionality of his name itself suggests that he might have been a freed slave. Ancient sources give Plautus's place of origin as Sarsina, Umbria, which if true indicates that he was tri-lingual in Greek, Latin and Umbrian.[8] The Plautine corpus (intertextually) demonstrates that the comic playwright read widely in Greek literature of various genres.[9]

We, like Roman scholars first starting to (re)construct their literary history in the first century BCE,[10] know none of the particulars of Plautus's life. The few dubious details that come down to us,[11] such as Aulus Gellius's claim in his late second-century CE *Attic Nights* that Plautus earned money 'in the occupation of stage-personnel' (3.3.14), can be marshalled in support of various scholarly 'narratives' of Plautus's life (low-status freed slave, non-Roman actor in native Italian drama, Greek actor touring with the Artists of Dionysus,[12] et al.). The accepted dates of Plautus's life, 254–184 BCE, if not exact, accurately reflect a comic career spanning the last years of the Second Punic War (218–201 BCE) down through the 190s and into the 180s BCE (see pp. 19–23). *Casina* is dated securely to *c.* 185 BCE by Myrrhina's reference to the Roman Senate's emergency ban of Bacchic worship in 186 BCE: as she reminds the fabricating Lysidamus near the play's end, 'There aren't any Bacchants revelling now!' (980).

The beginnings of drama and literature at Rome

Latin literature traditionally is said to begin in 240 BCE, when at least one play based on a Greek model was performed by Livius Andronicus at the Roman Festival (*Ludi Romani*) in honour of Jupiter that year. If the date is correct, this inaugural performance closely followed Rome's victory in the First Punic War (261–241 BCE) and its emergence as a Mediterranean military and geopolitical power. Other translations such as Livius Andronicus's of Homer's *Odyssey* soon followed. This fledgling literature in Latin, based on long-established literary genres of Greece, is thus inextricably bound with the enhancement of Roman nationalist identity and the acquisition of cultural capital.[13] Literature primarily flourished among the educated elite. At the same time, Roman legions stationed in Sicily and southern Italy during the war had been exposed to various Greek entertainments, including drama. Details are sketchy, but demand for Greek-inspired drama certainly increased in post-war Rome, and the city's politicians seized a new opportunity for self-promotion by sponsoring plays at state festivals. Playwright-translators also played a critical role in the establishment of theatrical shows in Rome based on Greek performances and scripts.[14] Plautus belongs to the second wave of Europe's first large-scale translation project.[15] As we shall see, Latin writers such as Plautus enthusiastically embraced the 'secondariness' of their translated literature and typically converted this into a creative asset; contemporary studies of Latin poetry now largely focus on unravelling its sophisticated dialogue with Greek literature.[16]

Plautus and Italian comic traditions

Plautus's fantastical name closely associates him – and his work – with mostly unscripted traditions of Italian drama. The term 'Atellan farce' reflects this ribald genre's origin in the town of Atella in Campania.[17] Only fragments of its first-century BCE literary form survive. In Plautus's time, Atellan farce consisted of itinerant performances featuring improvised skits by masked actors. These actors seem to have developed stock, endlessly repeatable situations, with a cast of five stereotypical characters: Bucco ('Fool'), Dossenus ('Glutton'), Manducus ('Jaws'), Pappus ('Grandpappy') and the ever-popular Maccus, who, like Bucco, was some sort of clown. Maccus appears to

have been a master-impersonator, as is suggested by extant titles of
farces such as 'Maccus the Soldier', 'The Twin Macci' and 'Maccus the
Virgin'. The last title suggests a mock marriage with cross-dressing as
in *Casina*.[18] What little we can glean from the scant evidence for
performances of Atellan farce suggests a non-elite world that admitted
obscene language, parody of various kinds, rustic situations and
manners, slapstick and comedic banter. Extant fragments of Atellan
farce show some of the same metres found in Plautine comedy, and
performances seem to have included singing and dancing. We cannot
determine if Plautus performed in Atellan farce, but his clan name
'Maccius' invites comparison of his plays with the improvisatory style
of Atellan farce.

Mime broadly describes Italian dramatic forms of 'low realism'.[19]
It survives only in its first-century BCE literary form through the
preserved fragments of Decimus Laberius and Publius Syrus. Unscripted performances of Italian mime, which predate Plautus, seem to
have featured vignettes of everyday life, sexual situations (especially
adultery), politics, literary and other forms of parody, and broad satire
of persons and institutions. The cast of characters includes such figures
as flatterers, slaves, adulterers and jealous husbands, and its settings
usually were low-status, for example the worlds of innkeepers and
fullers. Mime actors did not wear masks and performed barefoot rather
than in sandals or slippers. Troupes were itinerant, and their simple,
portable sets probably required only a small performance space. The
literary remains of mime suggest the use of spoken dialogue, song
and dance. Italian mime became notorious among Roman elites for its
obscenity and sexual explicitness; male actors wore exaggerated
phalluses and mime unusually employed female actors, who sometimes
stripped onstage. While Plautine comedy rarely, if ever, meets
anyone's definition of obscene, and sexual matters typically are treated
euphemistically, the family name 'Plautus' suggests some connection,
whether biographical or programmatic, between Plautine comedy and

Italian mime. One of Plautus's innovative treatments within the Greco-Roman genre of New Comedy is, for example, his amplification of the role of clever slave (*seruus callidus*) along with frequent representation of the demimonde of pimps, prostitutes, parasites et al., in which this trickster operates.

The reception of Greek comic theatre in Rome

Greek New Comedy, which flourished in Athens *c.* 325–250 BCE and today is represented primarily by the extant works of Menander, was cosmopolitan in its plots and characters, and so readily transferrable to other city-states.[20] In sharp contrast to the earlier Old Comedy, the exuberantly satirical comedy of fifth-century Athens that primarily survives in the plays of Aristophanes (died *c.* 385 BCE), Greek New Comedy is built around mundane conflicts arising from mistakes, misconceptions and ignorance between members of Athenian middle- to upper-class households. Greek New Comedy maintains unities of time and place and is neatly organized into five acts. Prominent features of Menander include naturalistic dialogue and skilled treatment of characters' emotional states and motivations. Old Comedy's musical variety and linguistic aggressiveness were all but muted in New Comedy. The exuberant chorus (often with animal identities and costumes) of Old Comedy is relegated to a non-integral performance between acts, simply marked '(song) of the chorus' in New Comedy texts. Menander overwhelmingly is in spoken iambics (about 85 per cent), the rest of the plays consisting mostly of musically accompanied and possibly chanted trochaics (there are only a few traces of other sung measures). While the domestic characters (for example slaves, fathers and sons, soldiers, prostitutes, cooks, the girl next door) and typically romantic plots of New Comedy are largely fixed, Menander privileges psychological realism and nuanced expression, especially in monologues. New Comedy's costumes and masks made characters appear more like real people than they had in Old Comedy. Dramatic illusion is usually preserved in extant Greek New Comedy, with characters only occasionally speaking directly to spectators as 'gentleman'. Menander's comedies typically move toward a predictably harmonious conclusion, often capped by a marriage; traditional family values, as also those of the Athenian *polis* in general, are thus ultimately upheld.[21] Little is known about Diphilus of Sinope (born *c.* 360–350 BCE), who provides Plautus with the source play, *Klēroumenoi* or *The Lot-drawers*, for *Casina*, as well as for his extant *Rudens*. Apart from Latin translations, Diphilus's work survives only in titles and fragments, which suggest a preference for mythical burlesque (cf. Plautus's *Amphitruo*), caricature over complex delineation of character, and perhaps bold theatrical effects.[22] New Comedy reached Italy by the mid-third century BCE through itinerant performances by Greek professional actors known as 'Artists of Dionysus'.[23]

Early Roman comic playwrights made Greek New Comedy the foundation of their own version of the genre, the *fabula palliata* or 'play in Greek dress'. Their adaptation of Greek New Comedy to Roman stages, however, was anything but slavish, as playwrights from the start seem to have radically restructured their Greek sources, in part due to the influence of native Italian dramatic traditions.[24] Roman comedy seems always to have been far more musical than its Greek predecessor. Only about one-third of all lines in Plautus are spoken (that is, in iambics), while the remainder of his comedies employ musically accompanied measures.[25] This large-scale musical stylization of Greek New Comedy by itself largely undermines the latter's prioritization of naturalism (at least to judge by Menander). Similarly, Greek New Comedy's five-act structure was eliminated, and Roman comedy instead features continuous action, with the stage only occasionally (and briefly) emptied of characters. Musical patterning seems largely to have replaced acts as the primary means of structuring

Roman comedies. In Plautus, the alternation between musically accompanied and unaccompanied scenes is paramount, where it is useful to speak of musical 'arcs'.[26] An arc is marked by a rise in tension in the spoken portions of plays ('inhalation') that is necessarily followed by a musical fall ('exhalation'). *Casina* consists of six musical arcs, each with its own crescendo and fall (not unlike an act), though detailed analysis of these is challenging, given our overall ignorance of Plautine music and its specific effects in performance.[27]

Athenian comedy belonged to religious and civic festivals and was funded both publicly and by the contributions of wealthy citizens. The venue of the annual dramatic competitions, the Theatre of Dionysus in Athens, grew to accommodate around 17,000 spectators, which included both citizens and foreigners. By comparison, early Roman theatre seems to have been a much simpler and ephemeral spectacle. Annual religious festivals in Rome included drama as well as other entertainments designed to honour gods.[28] Theatrical performances were also held on such special occasions as aristocratic funerals, a victorious general's fulfilment of a vow to a deity, or the inauguration of temples and religious cults. Unlike in Athens, there was neither a central venue for early Roman theatre, nor were performances dedicated to a single god of theatre. Roman festivals and other public occasions at which theatrical performances took place were state supported, and magistrates tasked with their organization provided additional funding. Very few details related to the production of festival performances are known: actor-managers, who headed acting troupes, probably negotiated contracts for plays and playwrights with magistrates.[29] A kind of stage-manager supplied troupes with costumes and props.[30] Though Roman theatre did not, as Greek New Comedy, respect a three-actor rule, acting troupes were small.[31] Whereas acting was a respected technical art in Greece, in Rome it was a very low-status profession that employed mostly slaves and former slaves.[32] We do not know how many plays were performed on a single occasion; the number of performances of an individual play might vary owing to the practice of *instauratio* or 'repetition' following some disruption of ritual procedure. We know nothing of the fate of theatrical scripts after performances, as the Roman state did not require official copies of these to be preserved (as the Athenian statesman Lycurgus prescribed for Greek tragedy in the fourth century BCE) and seems not to have kept theatrical records in Plautus's day. We must assume that Plautus's comedies underwent various alterations in the course of their written transmission; this of course was probably already true while he was active in theatre, as dramatic scripts invariably undergo changes every time they are performed. The twenty nearly complete comedies we possess today are thus perhaps best described as 'Plautine'.

Roman comedy's performance spaces – the Roman forum, the circus, temples – remained temporary until the dedication of Pompey's grand stone theatre in 55 BCE. For religious, moral and political reasons, the ruling elite resisted the construction of large, permanent theatrical venues in Rome, even after these were established throughout Italy.[33] The effect was to institutionalize theatre as a kind of 'gift' to the Roman people that depended on the Senate's and the individual magistrates' munificence each year.[34] These temporary (wooden) structures no doubt influenced how Greek New Comedy was adapted in Rome, though the lack of material remains for early Roman theatre hinders our understanding of this process, as we must rely solely on the extant texts for clues.[35] A painted backdrop (*scaena*) represented one to three houses, as in Greek New Comedy, through whose doors characters accessed the performance space (*proscaenium*). Characters also entered and exited by side wings, which led to either the forum/ city or the harbour/country. Unlike their Greek counterparts, early Roman theatres lacked an orchestra or dancing area. We know little of crowd capacities, but a 191 BCE debut performance of Plautus's *Pseudolus* before the temple of the Great Mother (Cybele) on the

Palatine Hill probably accommodated fewer than 2,000 spectators.[36] By 194 BCE, senators enjoyed the privilege of reserved seating next to the stage.[37] There was no curtain in early Roman theatre. These close confines made the performance space of early Roman theatre more permeable between actors and audiences than it had been in Greek New Comedy and perhaps is one of the reasons Plautus's characters frequently speak directly to spectators. The configurations of space, seating, sight lines and acoustics of temporary Roman theatre thus created a very different theatrical experience from that of spectators in Athens' monumental Theatre of Dionysus.

All the actors wore masks and costumes that were somehow codified by character type (slave, old man/father of the family, mother of the family, et al.), though regrettably little is known about these and how they might have differed (or not) from those used in Greek New Comedy.[38] In *Casina,* special provisions are made for Chalinus's costuming as a bride (**Scene 19**). Props are used to good effect by Plautus, as when in *Casina* an urn is brought on stage for the marriage lottery (**Scene 7**).[39] Lysidamus's walking stick becomes a semiotically charged prop as it changes hands in **Scenes 22–3** of *Casina* (see pp. 73–6, 85–6). There also was a god's altar somewhere on the Roman stage, which itself represented a street in front of the stage-houses. Finally, while later Roman theatre representations show enclosed porches attached to the *scaena* where eavesdroppers might lurk, there is no evidence for these in early Roman theatre, where eavesdroppers could make clear their intention to speak only to the audience through movements of their head/mask and body (as is the case for all asides in Plautus).[40]

Plautus, Latin translator and Roman playwright

The discovery and 1968 publication of 113 lines of Menander's *Dis Exapaton* or *The Double Deceiver,* Plautus's source for lines 494–562 of his *Bacchides*, now allow us to directly assess Plautus's translation and adaptation practices.[41] Comparative analysis of parallel sections of these comedies verifies that Plautus in the main follows the plot and action of Menander. Plautus sometimes translates closely or takes great liberties with his source, significantly transposing, curtailing or expanding verses of *The Double Deceiver* to suit the conventions of early Roman theatre or to serve his particular dramatic priorities. Plautus altogether eliminates two scenes of dialogue between young Sostratos and his father on each side of the act break in Menander. Following the first of these, the pair exit so that Sostratos can return money he has stolen from his father. By contrast, in Plautus, Mnesilochus (= Sostratos) in a monologue (500–25) decides to hand over the money, which he does offstage. But before Mnesilochus returns (530), Plautus inserts a brief entrance monologue by Mnesilochus's friend Pistoclerus (526–9) to avoid Mnesilochus's immediate reappearance and bridge the act break in keeping with Roman comedy's continuous action.

One of Plautus's most striking transformations of his source involves character names, which he typically makes more exotically Greek, rather than Latinizing them. Menander's generically designated slave Syros ('Syrian') is renamed Chrysalus ('Goldie') in *Bacchides*, where he becomes one of Plautus's most compelling clever slaves and the architect of metacomic mischief. The name inspires a series of bilingual jokes playing on both the Greek and Latin words for 'gold'.[42] Chrysalus even code-switches to execute such a pun ('Chrysalus needs *chrysō*', 240), and also plays on the similarity of his Greek name and the Latin word (*crux*) for 'torture',[43] a central preoccupation of Plautus's defiant clever slaves. Most striking of all is Chrysalus's boldly metacomic assertion, 'I don't care for those Parmenos[44] and Syruses who cheat their masters out of a few minae' (*Bac.* 649–50), where he not only denigrates his Menandrean counterpart Syros, but also seems to make a programmatic statement about Plautine comedy and its enlargement of the clever slave's role.

Even when Plautus is translating closely, he can produce significant alterations of his source text, as can be seen through comparison of *Dis Exapaton* 11–17 and *Bac.* 494–99. In both scenes Moschos's/Pistoclerus's father exhorts Sostratos/Mnesilochus to rebuke his own son for partying at the prostitute's house. Whereas the entire section of the papyrus is in spoken dialogue, Plautus drastically transforms the tone of the scene by casting it in longer, musically accompanied trochaics, whose diction seems comparatively artificial. Where Menander strives for natural conversation, Plautus is rhetorically exuberant and his characters' emotions are heightened. The two monologues diverge significantly in tone, purpose and effect. The Menandrean monologue is a psychological tour de force that captures Sostratos's emotional crisis and forces spectators to sympathize with him. Mnesilochus's corresponding monologue in Plautus, which doubles the length of its source, features very different registers of language and sentiment; his speech aims more at rhetorically dazzling spectators than winning their sympathy for himself as it marks him out as yet another of Plautus's foolish and maudlin young men in love.

Bac. 540–51 survive in only one of the two strands of the play's Latin transmission, but the German scholar Leo,[45] writing before the 1968 discovery of the papyrus, asserted that these lines had to be genuine precisely because they are so Menandrean! While the 1968 publication of *The Double Deceiver* fragment surprisingly proved that Leo was wrong about these lines being added by Plautus, the observation that Plautus here produces dialogue whose features (moralizing, dramatic tension and exploitation of misunderstanding) closely recall Menander is correct. It may be the case that Plautus has here introduced and translated a passage from somewhere else in Menander,[46] or the Roman comic playwright may be demonstrating that he can outdo Menander at his own game. In either case, this instance of literary *imitatio* ('imitation') and *aemulatio* ('rivalry') would be evident only to cognoscenti in Plautus's audience who knew

Menander in Greek. Nonetheless, Plautus's competitive poetic spirit vis-à-vis his Greek predecessor is unquestionable.

Plautus's *Casina*: translation, metacomedy and metapoetics

The complete loss of Diphilus's *The Lot-drawers*, Plautus's source for *Casina*, prevents us from performing any comparative analysis of it with *Casina*, but we nonetheless can make some conjectures about how Plautus refashioned his Greek source text. Plautus obviously has transformed Diphilus's play into a much more musical comedy: some 35 per cent of *Casina*'s verses are spoken, with the rest being musically accompanied, most within complex songs. Plautus in his usual playful manner has enlarged various verbal effects, such as alliteration and assonance, and no doubt rhetorically amplified his source through the deployment of such figures as metaphor, hyperbole and metonymy. And Plautus, as *Casina* demonstrates, is a master of the parody of various linguistic registers (for example, legal, bureaucratic, tragic).

Language enjoys fresh treatment in Plautus, where its expressive and semantic capacities are constantly extended and renewed. Plautine characters creatively employ metaphors and similes to persuade auditors to their point of view and perhaps even force them to look at things in a new, 'translated' way. Through tortuous farm-labour and forced sexual voyeurism, Olympio promises to transform Chalinus into 'a horse's crupper' (125) and reduce him to 'a mouse trapped inside a wall' (140); the despondent Lysidamus pledges to 'make a cushion out of his sword' (307) by falling on it; and Olympio accuses the cook's crew of being 'thorns' (720) because of their alleged propensity for grabbing on to things to steal.[47] Chalinus calls the momentarily puffed up Olympio a 'magnet for cattle-prods' (447) to signal his comeuppance and the likelihood of tortuous punishment.

Already in antiquity Plautus was renowned for his verbal coinages, as when Lysidamus creates a neologism in dubbing Olympio his 'co-husband' (797), Pardalisca refers to her female accomplices as 'gourmandesses' (778), and when Lysidamus invents incongruous diminutives to address Chalinus, now disguised as the bride Casina, as 'my robust little one' (852) and 'my pretty little pretty' (854). Sexual matters in Plautus are expressed in vivid euphemisms, as in Chalinus's description of Lysidamus's aggressive sexual advances toward Olympio: 'I do believe he wants to burrow into the farm-manager's bladder' (455). Puns operate on virtually every page of Plautus. When Lysidamus, for example, requests that Olympio purchase sole (Latin *solea* can denote both the fish and sandals) for the wedding feast, the eavesdropping Chalinus in an aside (495–6) states his preference for pounding the old man's face with cheap wooden clogs. Through all this verbal inventiveness and play, Plautine language itself becomes a kind of trope for the translation process, as well as more broadly hinting at new ways of viewing experience – that is, everything need not be what convention and habit make it out to be.

While Plautus's characters speak and sing in extremely lively Latin, their social world is a strange conglomerate of Greek and Roman. Characters with impressive Greek names and who are costumed as Greeks[48] always use the Latin names of the Olympian gods (Jupiter, Juno, Venus, et al.) while simultaneously peppering their speech with Greek exclamations and other Greek loan-words that support the illusion of an Athenian setting. For example, in his first appearance in *Casina*, when the infatuated and possibly besotted Lysidamus confesses that, to make himself more attractive to Casina, he has been frequenting 'perfumers', he uses the Greek word *myropolas* (226; cf. 238). In putting on airs as a bridegroom, the servile Olympio pompously breaks out into Greek (**Scene 15**), though in this same context he also describes himself as 'walking in a [Roman] patrician style' (723a). In *Casina*'s denouement, Myrrhina tags the exposed

Lysidamus's behaviour as markedly un-Roman ('he was bedding [*moechissat*] Casina', 976) by using a Greek verb that is extant only here in Latin. Domesticating 'Romanizations' are interspersed throughout the play: for example, in her duet with Cleostrata, Myrrhina repeats the Roman divorce formula ('out of the house, woman!', 211–12); Cleostrata scorns Alcesimus as 'the pillar of the [Roman] senate, the sentinel of the people' (536); and coopting official language Olympio describes his management of Lysidamus's farm as his 'governorship' (110). Plautus thus never attempts to fully represent 'Rome' onstage, but the dissonant, hybrid world of *Casina*, as that of any Plautine comedy, can best be described as 'Plautinopolis'.[49] Plautus thus is a highly visible translator of his Greek sources,[50] who, we shall see, also exploits the theatricality of his comedies to position himself within the tradition of New Comedy taken over from Greece.

The pervasive deployment of metacomic effects is in fact a distinctive feature of Plautine comedy, with *Casina* presenting a particularly sophisticated example. During Pardalisca's messenger speech describing Casina's fictional rampage inside (**Scene 14**), the frightened Lysidamus is made to exclaim, 'There isn't and never has been an old man in love [*senex amator*] as wretched as me' (684–5), where he refers to both his stock character and inept performance in this role. Pardalisca in an aside then congratulates herself for her convincing narrative:

> I'm playing [*ludo*] him quite cleverly!
> Everything I just told him was complete fiction:
> My mistress and the neighbour lady here conceived this trick,
> And I was sent out to play [*ludere*] him!
>
> 685–8

As Latin *ludus* describes amusement in general and in the plural *ludi* denotes festivals such as the one in which *Casina* is performed, Pardalisca here confirms that Cleostrata and Myrrhina have already started to conduct a scheme that amounts to a play-within-the-play. This conceit becomes more explicit when Pardalisca declares the great athletic festivals (*ludi*) of Greece to be no match for the 'playful games' (*ludi ludificabiles*, 761) to be performed at Lysidamus's and Olympio's expense. Myrrhina further clarifies that the faux-wedding, with its elaborate costuming and formal presentation of the bride, is a performance whose aftermath the women will witness as an internal audience: 'we've come out on the street here to watch the wedding games' (*ludos . . . nuptialis*, 856).

Clever Plautine metapoetics may underlie the unusual amount of attention in *Casina* bestowed upon Lysidamus's cloak, his *pallium*, the outer garment worn by most male characters in Roman comedy that gave the genre its name, (*fabula*) *palliata*.[51] Lysidamus first draws attention to his cloak when, to conceal his amorous intentions from Cleostrata, he uses it to wipe off his heavily perfumed hair oil (237). He does not fool his wife, who notes that the cloak is wrinkled (246), which Cleostrata takes as evidence he has been in a brothel. Pardalisca, as part of her over-the-top performance as a paratragic messenger, next draws special attention to the old man's cloak when she mockingly asks him to fan her with it (637). The old man ultimately loses his *pallium* in his offstage sexual tussle with Chalinus, as he himself points out to the audience in his desperate appeal to them: 'Poor me! I've been *de-cloaked*' (945).[52] Lacking any remains of Diphilus's *The Lot-drawers*, scholars have long conducted detective-like searches to speculate about Plautus's alterations to his source. Lysidamus's cloak perhaps provides an overlooked clue toward solving an unsolvable puzzle. If the faux-wedding and its aftermath that conclude *Casina* are Plautus's doing, the loss of Lysidamus's cloak[53] metonymically points to Plautus's creative transformation of his source: a conventional recognition scene (*anagnorisis*), in which Casina was discovered to be free-born, and wedding-finale in Diphilus have not been adapted into the Latin version and have been replaced by the farcical fiasco that now renders Lysidamus cloakless onstage, in a situation that recalls the bawdiness of Atellan farce or Italian mime more than Greek New Comedy. When Cleostrata asks Lysidamus what happened to his *pallium* (975, 978), the desperate old man attempts to blame Bacchants, the frenetic female worshippers of Bacchus (see pp. 32–4), for its loss but Myrrhina quickly interjects that Bacchants no longer 'revel/play' (*ludunt*, 980). Myrrhina here suggests that Lysidamus's attempt to scapegoat the Bacchants is a ridiculous drama of his own making; in *Casina* the exposed old man's punishment in the women's internal play calls for him to lose his characteristic Greek costume and undergo the public shame of appearing in his underwear before his wife and spectators. In a characteristically Plautine move, Cleostrata then generates a pun on the discarded *pallium* by noting that the nearly naked Lysidamus is 'pale' (*palles*, 982). To bring Plautus's comedy to an end and restore the domestic status-quo, the cloak, along with his walking stick, ultimately is returned to Lysidamus (1008).

Another motif with seemingly programmatic significance in *Casina* is the idea of novelty, as this is repeatedly articulated through the adjective *nouus* ('new').[54] In *Casina*, 'new' overwhelmingly refers to the bride in the play, whether in the traditional sense 'newlywed', or, with reference to the faux-marriage, with such connotations as 'strange', 'unprecedented', 'inventive'.[55] The prologue speaker prominently introduces this notion when he characterizes the marriage plot involving slaves as something 'new' (70). While spectators at this point do not know exactly what sort of marriage lies ahead,[56] the prologue speaker is prepping them for the faux wedding between the male slaves in *Casina*. At this point, spectators seemingly are only being asked to accept some imaginative leap that may subvert their notion of traditional marriage. Such emphasis on the novelty of Chalinus as the bride Casina again supports the theory that the homosexual wedding may be Plautus's addition to Diphilus's play. In the case of highly stereotyped New Comedy, more experienced theatregoers no doubt sought assurances that they were about to see something 'new', that is, some variation(s) on the genre's formulaic plots and characters. The wedding plot intriguingly promises to deliver in this regard. The prologue speaker in fact has already promised novelty more generally, when he insists that Plautus has 'written [*The Lot-drawers*] anew in Latin' (33–4) and then proceeds to drop further hints about specific innovations Plautus has introduced.[57] In this way Plautus claims that, despite the 'secondariness' of his literary task, his appropriation of Greek New Comedy, in his richly creative translation, introduction of lively elements from Italian drama, and overall infusion of his idiosyncratic sensibility, necessarily involves the creation of something fresh.

The Social-Historical Context

Casina falls within a dynamic period of Roman history following the Second Punic War. While this was a pivotal moment in Roman imperialism and (inter)nationalism, expansion also brought significant changes to the city-state's everyday life. Some of Rome's growing pains and social tensions can be glimpsed in *Casina*, as the play centres on a comic family whose interpersonal relationships often reflect broader areas of contemporary Roman life, including militarism, slavery, religion and women's roles and rights.

The post-Second Punic War world of *Casina*

Rome's victory in its first conflict with Carthage signalled its emergence as a city-state to be reckoned with in Mediterranean politics (see pp. 3–4). The Second Punic War (218–201 BCE), in which Hannibal terrorized Italy and threatened Roman security until his decisive defeat by Scipio at the Battle of Zama in 202 BCE, more definitively marks the beginnings of Roman imperialism. Plautus's dramatic career corresponds closely with this stage of Roman expansion, during which the Romans defeated the Carthaginians, Macedonians and other Greeks and their allies in a series of wars extending into the 180s BCE that brought enormous benefits, both material and symbolic, to the triumphant city of Rome.[1] The Romans' steady, large-scale acquisition of territories, enslaved persons and new wealth thus forms the political, military and social backdrop of Plautus's comedies. The early second-century BCE city-state of Rome, though still far from administering an empire via permanently stationed legions and complex bureaucracy, increasingly found itself engaged in international relations and the everyday business of its new subject territories. Rome's ascendancy to Mediterranean superpower status also brought social-historical transformations at home, including the influx of not only foreigners, but new customs, especially from the Greek world. The increased wealth of the enslavers also came with new opportunities for social mobility for the enslaved, as some slaves over time earned their freedom and became Roman citizens.[2] There were inevitable 'culture wars', as long-standing tradition and social innovations collided, putting stress and strain on Roman political, religious, legal and other institutions. Though Plautus rarely alludes to specific events or persons of this period, the topical matters of the newly multicultural city permeate the comedies.[3] As a comic playwright, Plautus perhaps unsurprisingly does not clearly take sides on contemporary issues, though his characters engage extensively in what can be termed the public discourse of post-Second Punic War Rome.[4]

Plautus's comic appropriation of the words and deeds of Roman militarism, power and administrative control can be glimpsed throughout *Casina*, where these may metaphorically assume thematic significance. For example, both Olympio and Chalinus grandiosely refer to the former's management of Lysidamus's farm as the 'governorship' (99, 110) of his 'province' (103), where Olympio has formally been assigned tasks in the manner of a Roman magistrate (100). Olympio extends this administrative conceit so far as to claim that in coming to town he has formally appointed a curator of the farm in his absence (104–5). Each of the slaves stakes a competitive claim to Casina as his (war) 'booty'.[5] When Olympio wins the lottery for Casina, the farm-manager incongruously declares that he has prevailed 'because of [his] *pietas* and that of [his] ancestors' (418). Olympio thus defies the Roman legal fiction that slaves had no parents, let alone ancestors, to attribute his random success in the lottery to his distinguished family pedigree! The farm-manager here perhaps humorously calls to mind the ubiquitous self-promotion of generals (*imperatores*), who in this period typically cite aristocratic privilege as part of their pitches to celebrate grand military triumphs in Rome.[6] Olympio's pretensions to inherited glory in connection with his temporarily successful acquisition of Casina will of course painfully crash later in the play. In *Casina* the technical term for a Roman magistrate's power – *imperium* (later 'empire') – is reserved for the women: when, during the lottery scene, Olympio complains to Lysidamus of being pummelled by Chalinus at Cleostrata's prompting, the old man advises forbearance because, in his marriage, 'my wife displays the power' (409). In Pardalisca's parodic marriage instructions to the bride Chalinus, she urges that the wife's 'voice and power' prevail and that, while a husband's role is to provide, a wife's is to 'plunder' him (821–2). The marital and martial here neatly converge.

The prologue speaker introduces *Casina*'s recurrent motif of military combat: 'both father and son are now secretly preparing troops against each other' (50–1) in what will be a war by proxies (52–7), Olympio the farm-manager and Chalinus, who is described as Euthynicus's military assistant.[7] The play's real battle is between spouses, as becomes clear in Cleostrata's opening song: 'I'll take my revenge against lover-boy (that disgrace to the human race!) with hunger, thirst, sharp words and sharp treatment' (155–6). Lysidamus repeatedly casts his incompetent and doomed scheme to win Casina as a military-style campaign, as when at the start of the lottery for Casina he commands Chalinus 'to bring the battle standards closer and charge' (357; cf. 352). Cleostrata promises Chalinus victory and Olympio miserable defeat (403) just before a physical skirmish erupts at the climactic moment of the lottery; when Lysidamus orders Olympio to strike Chalinus in the face (404), and Cleostrata has Chalinus respond in kind (407), Olympio describes his own face as having been assailed (412). In the lottery's aftermath, Chalinus admits defeat in an aside, and adds that he is especially aggrieved by Lysidamus's undue interest in the outcome (428–33). He shortly changes his tune ('losers will soon be winners', 510) after overhearing Lysidamus's and Olympio's specific plans concerning Casina. The last word on achieving victory in the play again belongs to the women, when Pardalisca exhorts the bride Chalinus: 'may your power outpower your husband's and may you dominate him and become his dominatrix' (*tuaque ut potior pollentia sit uincasque uirum uictrixque sies*, 819–20). All war in *Casina* ceases once Chalinus prevails in the farcical honeymoon. There Chalinus defends himself against Olympio's ill-fated attempt to sexually penetrate him through a successful 'blockade' of the region Olympio believes defines women (921–2), and, after piercing Olympio with his beard, Chalinus completely overcomes him in violent foot-to-chest combat (929–31a). The defeated Olympio reports having then fled the scene (932), only to face his current public disgrace. A further dimension of a sexual power struggle can be charted through the role of swords in the play.[8]

Finally, there are instances in *Casina* where issues of Roman national(ist) identity arise. The prologue speaker, following the convention of 'valediction' in Plautine prologues, closes his thus: 'Be well, good luck and keep winning victories through your true valour, as you always have before' (87–8). Reprising his opening theme of *Fides*/trust (see p. 36), the prologue speaker credits the warriors in the audience with 'honest valour',[9] which he suggests is an essential national trait behind Rome's recent history of military success. Such an assertion, while aimed at eliciting collective pride among spectators, again echoes the claims of elite generals competing for the right to celebrate a triumph, and so more generally evokes the competitive, individualistic ethos of the incipient empire. The lowly farm-manager of *Casina* also incongruously participates in contemporary discourse on 'Roman-ness'. While Olympio obviously is putting on airs when he tells the cooks he has 'no stomach for barbarian slop' (747–7a), his use of the loaded term 'barbarian'[10] invites comparative evaluation of Greek and Roman cuisine and, more broadly, culture: who is the barbarian here, the actor speaking Latin in a Plautine comedy or the Greek character who, from a Roman perspective, reflexively deems everything non-Greek inferior? It is difficult to sort through the ironies here, but Plautus clearly has made the farm-manager enter the culture wars.[11]

Casina in the context of Roman marriage and family

Rome had a myth explaining the introduction of women to society and the establishment of marriage practice. The Roman historian Livy (59 BCE–17 CE) records that the newly created city of Rome was without women, and the Romans' neighbours scorned King Romulus's offer of an alliance through intermarriage (Livy 1.9–13). The Romans then invited the neighbouring Sabines to a festival with the intention of abducting their young women. In Livy's account, Romulus and his fellow citizens eventually win over the hearts of their abducted wives. When war between the Romans and Sabines erupts, the women heroically interpose themselves between the opposed lines of their fathers and husbands. The Sabine women declare that they prefer death to being either widowed or orphaned, in this way dramatically demonstrating their willingness to sacrifice their lives at a most critical moment at Rome's beginning.[12] The men cease hostilities and unite in enduring solidarity. The myth illustrates how Roman women are defined in relationship to their male guardians and how marriage in a patriarchal society is conceived as a transfer of women from fathers to husbands.

The oft-stated purpose of Roman marriage was the production of legitimate children.[13] Through procreation, Roman parents passed their citizenship on to the next generation and preserved the family line and name. Marriage in the Roman world was a private affair between families, with the state involved primarily in legal matters related to distribution of property, inheritance and the like. It is useful to keep in mind that throughout the history of Roman unions 'marriage for the most part was governed by customary rules rather than formal law'.[14] The family was headed by its father (*paterfamilias*), who by traditional sanction held absolute power over the household, which usually included his wife, their children, slaves, freedmen and freedwomen and any other dependents. The patriarch's power (*patria potestas*) was only theoretically unlimited, as in cases involving his right to put his children to death with impunity; in reality, the *paterfamilias*'s actions were always subject to social norms, unwritten rules, family custom and approval of peers.[15]

The two families of *Casina*, though nominally Athenian, are easily assimilable to Roman experience. Euthynicus is the single son (and perhaps only child) of Lysidamus and Cleostrata, a fact we learn from Lysidamus's childish insistence that his only son should agree to his wish – as his son's only father – to marry Casina to Olympio (263–4). Casina was exposed at birth by the neighbours, presumably, spectators would assume, because Alcesimus chose not to formally acknowledge a baby girl. We get no sense in *Casina* that Myrrhina and Alcesimus have any other children. As the wives and husbands of each seemingly affluent family are on close personal terms with each other, a marriage arrangement between the two families seems almost inevitable, as is to happen between Euthynicus and Casina after the play. While the power to arrange marriages ultimately rested with patriarchs, there is evidence that mothers had a say in the matter of choosing mates for their children. Cleostrata thus appears to conform with common practice in pushing for a match between Chalinus and Casina in the farcical slave marriage (259–61), where she actually is advocating on behalf of her son. Cleostrata's motives at any rate are obviously more just than her husband's, who seeks Casina only for sexually exploitative purposes.

At sixteen, Casina is of a typical age for marriage among Roman elites (girls only needed to be at least twelve). Since males tended to marry in their mid to late twenties, the audience may assume that the absent Euthynicus, in sharp contrast to his father,[16] also is at an appropriate age for marriage with Casina. Plautus playfully hints that Lysidamus in his perverse fantasies aims at concubinage with Casina (even though Roman men seem not to have simultaneously been legally married and in such a quasi-marital relationship). To placate Olympio's fears about his fate once Lysidamus dies, the old man asserts, 'your situation's better than you think if we win and I get to sleep with Casina' (338–9). Here the Latin jingle *cum Casina cubem* ('sleep with Casina') suggests *concubina* ('concubine', lit. 'a female one lies with').[17] Pardalisca in her fictional messenger's speech echoes Lysidamus's phrase and foreshadows the violent honeymoon scene with Chalinus: '[Casina] swore she'd kill the man she sleeps with tonight' (*quicum cubaret*, 671).[18] Myrrhina accuses the old man of such aspirations when she calls him a 'bigamist' near the play's end (974; see p. 75). Lysidamus's dream of concubinage with Casina is forever shattered by the blows he suffers at Chalinus's hands in their marriage bed.[19]

There were two forms of marriage available for Roman women: marriage that included the transfer of a father's power over his daughter to her husband (*cum manu*, 'with power') and marriage in which a woman remained under her father's guardianship in her marriage (*sine manu*, 'without power'). In a *cum manu* marriage, the older, more traditional preference, a new bride effectively found herself in the same legal position as a daughter of her husband. She could inherit a part of her husband's estate equal to that of his children, but like the latter – theoretically at least – was subject to her husband's absolute power within the household. In this asymmetrical relationship, a married

woman seems not to have been able to initiate divorce in Plautus's
time (this prohibition had disappeared by the end of the first century
BCE). By contrast, a woman who remained in her father's power after
her marriage retained ownership of any property she brought with her
to the marriage and retained her right to inheritance within the clan
into which she was born.[20] This latter, *sine manu* type of marriage, in
which a new bride remained a member of her natal family, seems to
have been gaining a foothold in the post-Second Punic War period as
a means of preserving familial holdings.[21] It is unclear what further,
if any, practical benefits *sine manu* marriage brought a woman (for
example, could her status be leveraged for increased personal freedom
or power?), since her ultimate guardian was her father, not the husband
with whom she lived.

Both Cleostrata and Myrrhina in *Casina* appear to be living in a
Roman *cum manu* arrangement,[22] and so entirely under their husbands'
legal control, as becomes evident in the riveting duet (**Scene 3**) in
which they discuss Cleostrata's marital situation. To Myrrhina's polite
query about her friend's grim expression, Cleostrata responds, 'That's
how it is for all women in bad marriages' (174–5), thereby inviting
spectators to consider her predicament as a societal trend. Before
divulging the specific cause of her aggravation, Cleostrata continues,
'My husband treats me in the worst way, and there's no way for me to
exercise my rights' (189–90).[23] In other words she cannot initiate
a divorce, and without any legal recourse can only complain to her
neighbour as she does now (cf. 162). Cleostrata soon reveals that
Lysidamus is in her opinion inappropriately demanding that Casina
be given in marriage to Olympio, to which she objects because she has
raised the girl at her own expense and also is aware of her husband's
sexual designs on the girl (193–5a). Myrrhina offers legally correct
and cautious commentary: a wife in a *cum manu* arrangement
technically can own nothing ('In my opinion, all that's yours is your
husband's', 202) and any claim to the contrary opens her up to charges

of sexual impropriety or theft (200–2). Myrrhina, here toeing the line of stern traditionalism, accordingly urges her friend to tolerate Lysidamus's behaviour as long as he adequately provides for her basic household needs (204–7) – that is, unless she is willing to risk hearing her husband utter the Roman divorce formula, 'out of the house, woman' (210–12). Cleostrata's objection that Myrrhina here is advocating against her own marital interests (208–9) suggests that she is much less willing than her friend to follow tradition and the letter of the law. At this point Cleostrata does not have a chance to elaborate on what she may have in mind for dealing with her current situation, as Lysidamus is seen approaching and the women's discussion abruptly ends (213).

Interestingly, we hear nothing of Cleostrata's dowry in *Casina*, even though 'the most common type of *matrona* in Plautine comedy is the *uxor dotata* ['dowered wife'] or *femina irata* ['angry woman'], the independently wealthy, nagging, shrewish counterpart to the besotted elderly patriarch'.[24] Dowries were traditional in either form of Roman marriage, and generally intended to support a husband's maintenance of his wife during a marriage. A 230 BCE law made provisions for the return or forfeiture of a dowry in the event of divorce, in which process a wife's or husband's alleged misconduct was relevant.[25] The conditions and circumstances related to the dowry and the prospect of its return no doubt were clearly articulated in a pre-marriage contract, but the possibility of a husband's having to return the initial capital his wife brought with her to the marriage might actually have afforded women some leverage in their dealings with their husbands – hence the comic stereotype of the dowered wife in Plautus – especially if a husband has spent or otherwise invested the dowry.[26] Plautus, however, in *Casina* refrains from raising any spectre of a dowry lurking behind Cleostrata's and Lysidamus's marital relationship. Apart from the issue of who owns Casina and Cleostrata's warning about squandering money to Lysidamus (248), we hear virtually nothing about household economics, which perhaps invites us to think more about other aspects of the couple's marriage (for example, emotional, personal, sexual). By not casting Cleostrata in the negative light of the dowered wife, the play seems to champion her cause, at least within the narrow circumstances of her husband's ridiculous lust for Casina.

Women's rights and prerogatives in post-Hannibalic War Rome

While free Roman women were classified as citizens, few opportunities for personal or professional development and no prerogatives of power were attached to their citizenship. Women in the Roman Republic could not participate in public life, vote in assemblies, serve in the military or hold any of the prestigious public offices to which men aspired. The extent of their education depended entirely on their male guardians' will, as there were no mandatory public schools for either boys or girls. Girls primarily were expected to marry, bear children and as wives conduct their household responsibilities.[27] The Punic Wars, however, brought social disruption and change, including within Roman households. The increasing length of military campaigns during the Second Punic War (sometimes up to six years for some legions), as obviously the death or enslavement of male guardians, no doubt forced some women to assume extraordinary duties, including even business and legal transactions.[28] We also catch glimpses of women's public demonstrations during the prolonged war against Hannibal and the Carthaginians. Following a disastrous Carthaginian ambush and the massacre of thousands of Roman legionnaires at Lake Trasimene, Italy, in 217 BCE, women demanding information about the battle and news of loved ones took to the streets of Rome and ultimately gathered at the city gates en masse

(Livy 22.7.1–14). This large-scale, highly visible public assembly was not tantamount to an anti-war protest per se, but it demonstrated the women's capability to remind senators and other authorities charged with the war's execution that it held grave consequences for the soldiers' wives and children, quite apart from the state's imperialistic designs or the ambitions of generals.[29]

Rome's state religion offered limited opportunities for public participation in cult by elite women. Most of the city's official cults were administered by male priests, but a few priestesses, such as the Vestal Virgins, enjoyed a strong civic presence, and there were a few exclusive women's festivals. Because Romans often looked to religious remedies in times of national crisis, there was a marked upswing in cult activity (such as new deities, temples and rituals) as Hannibal's formidable army threatened the city. As a result, participation in public worship by Roman women increased. The cult of Venus of Eryx in Sicily was introduced to Rome after the debacle at Lake Trasimene, as also later the worship of the Great Mother (Cybele) from Asia Minor (204 BCE). The Second Punic War precipitated reinvigorated worship of Juno in Rome.[30] In the wake of dire events and prodigies in 217 BCE, accelerated efforts to appease the goddess, one of whose great cult centres was Carthage, were marked by an especially grand procession to her temple (as Juno Regina) on the Aventine Hill. Women played a central and very public role in this elaborate renewal of Juno's cult, with some *matronae* appointed to fund the effort from their dowries (Livy 27.37.1–13). This boost in Juno's importance in Roman worship may subtly influence the audience of *Casina*'s perception of Cleostrata when she is referred to as 'Juno' in play, by both Lysidamus (230) and Chalinus (408). At any rate, the increased involvement of women in religious activity during the Second Punic War no doubt helped forge new relationships and networks among Roman women, in addition to encouraging further participation in civic and public business more generally. Roman women in this period may also have increased their engagement with forms of worship outside the sanction of state religion, such as the cult of Bacchus (see pp. 32–4).

Of particular relevance to *Casina* is a women's protest against the Oppian Law in 195 BCE. After a devastating loss of Roman manpower at the Battle of Cannae in 215 BCE, this extraordinary measure (the *Lex Oppia* of 215) limiting conspicuous consumption by Roman women was enacted. The law restricted women to possession of no more than a half ounce of gold, and prohibited their wearing multicoloured garments in public or riding in animal-drawn carriages inside the city or within a mile's radius of it, with an exception granted for participation in religious ritual.[31] This Second Punic War measure clearly was not passed for economic reasons, as the restrictions could bring no real benefit to the state treasury, but belongs to a long tradition of Roman sumptuary laws aimed at promoting the appearance of equality in a society marked by enormous disparities of wealth and power.[32]

In the secure and economically prosperous years immediately after Hannibal's defeat, public opinion regarding the Oppian Law seems to have shifted. In 195 BCE a movement to repeal these restrictions on women's expenditures gained momentum. With two tribunes in support of the repeal and two others seeking to retain the law, vigorous public debate ensued. Roman women lined the city streets leading to the forum and implored men as they passed by to revoke the law. Their demonstration of solidarity lasted several days and attracted growing support, as many women from Rome and its environs seem to have ignored appeals from their male guardians not to join the peacefully protesting crowds (Livy 34.1.5). According to Livy, the arch-traditionalist Cato the Elder spoke firmly against repeal of the law, arguing that the women's brash public protests were symptomatic of a larger threat to male authority, and that the women had no right to engage in any business, private let alone state-related, without the close supervision of their guardians (Livy 34.2–4). In support of the opposing view, Lucius Valerius Flaccus asserted that the restricted items and activities constituted badges of honour for Roman women, who were barred from public life, wherein men might hold office, prestigious priesthoods and military posts, and even celebrate triumphs. In an age of unprecedented male self-assertion in the public sphere, why should Roman women be deprived of their status symbols (Livy 34.7.8)?[33] The women's cause ultimately prevailed after they besieged the homes of the two tribunes who opposed the repeal.

The broad cultural conversation about women's property and power to which these events surrounding repeal of the *Lex Oppia* attest surface in Plautine comedy before *Casina*. In *Aulularia* or *The Pot of Gold* (*c.* 190 BCE), for example, the wealthy bachelor Megadorus complains at length (475–536) of the financial demands imposed on husbands by their richly dowered wives.[34] In his rant, which at times recalls the speech of Cato the Elder against repeal of the Oppian Law, Megadorus includes a lively impersonation of a dowered wife:[35]

> No woman can then say: 'I have brought you a dowry
> That far exceeds the money you had.
> It is only fair then that I receive purple and gold objects,
> Maids, mule-cart drivers, and man-slaves,
> And slaves to convey greetings, and carriages to convey me.'
>
>   498–502

Some items here directly recall the *Lex Oppia*, and the dowered wife's demand for maids (*ancillas*, 261) brings to mind the situation of *Casina*, where Cleostrata argues with Lysidamus about the general supervision of her maids (261) and her claim to ownership of Casina in particular.[36] Similar discussion permeates Plautus's *Poenulus* or *The Little Carthaginian*, usually dated to sometime after *Aulularia* and probably before *Casina*.[37] What is clear then is that the controversies about women's rights as these relate to property and, by extension, the role of women within families were still current at the time of *Casina*'s first production. A discussion such as that between Cleostrata and Myrrhina in **Scene 3** thus went straight to the heart of lively contemporary debate on marriage (see pp. 23–8, 43–4).

The Bacchic scandal of 186 BCE and *Casina*

At a critical moment in the denouement of *Casina*, Lysidamus, Cleostrata and Myrrhina have a brief but culturally and thematically resonant exchange about the cult of Bacchus:

> Lys. As Hercules is my witness, my dear, some Bacchants – Cleo.
> Bacchants?
> Lys. Yes, Bacchants, my dear wife – Yes, Bacchants for sure – Myrrh.
> That's
> nonsense and he knows it! There aren't any Bacchic rites now!
>
> 979–80

Myrrhina's insistence that there no longer are Bacchic revels allows us to date the play to sometime after 186 BCE, the year of the Senate's brutal suppression of Bacchic worship in Rome and throughout Italy, and before Plautus's death in 184. Our chief source for this unusual event (the Romans typically tolerated the introduction of foreign religious cults) again is Livy, who provides a long and very lively account.[38] Livy relates an elaborate plot involving a virtuous son, an evil stepfather and a virtuous prostitute named Hispala Faecenia that produced shocking allegations of nefarious cult activity, ranging from poisonings to murders committed to the beat of drums and clash of cymbals during nocturnal rituals. The Roman authorities' investigation further revealed reports of women and men inappropriately consorting, freeborn boys being sexually corrupted, orgies, homosexuality and other allegations of frenzied cult activity. While Livy no doubt embellishes some details in his engagingly literary account, an inscription on a bronze tablet found in Italy generally confirms what the historian reports to be the dire consequences of the Senate's emergency decree: sharp restrictions on the initiates' right to assemble were instituted, shrines were demolished and priests rounded up throughout Italy. Those accused of crimes were summarily executed, including women, who were turned over to their male guardians for punishment, or in the absence of these were executed by the state. The motivations for the Senate's unprecedented crackdown are debated, and many scholars are sceptical that the cult posed such a real threat to Roman state religion or the general public order as suggested by Livy's rhetorically amplified narrative. The Senate, for example, may simply have found a convenient scapegoat through which to reassert its authority that was threatened in an age of ambitious individuals.[39]

Evidence for the general perception of Bacchic cult can be found in references scattered across Plautine comedy. In *Amphitruo*, a slave suggests that his master's confused wife, the unwitting victim of Jupiter's impersonation of her husband, suffers from Bacchic madness (703–4). Elsewhere, a cook who has been physically assaulted compares his (male) attacker to a raving Bacchant (*Aul.* 408); a tutor calls the prostitutes he believes are corrupting his charge 'bloodsucking Bacchants' (*Bac.* 371–2); and a character feigning madness invokes Bacchus (*Men.* 835). These casual references to the cult as a locus of insanity, irrationality and violence reflect what probably was a condemnatory popular perception of the cult among non-initiates (and perhaps helps to explain why the Senate had no qualms about suppressing the cult so brutally). This communal perception of the cult perhaps also informs the notion of a sword-wielding Casina raging inside Lysidamus's house as reported in Pardalisca's messenger's speech (**Scene 14**), at least to a listener like Lysidamus who does not grasp that Pardalisca's account is entirely fictional. The full import of the deeply ironic scene is only realized in the final revelation that the

phallically-driven Lysidamus is the play's true Bacchant. When
Cleostrata presses the publicly disgraced Lysidamus to account for his
lost cloak, the *senex* attempts to place blame on Bacchants.[40] Myrrhina
cuts off his ridiculous explanation in mid-sentence: 'That's nonsense
and he knows it, there certainly aren't any Bacchic women revelling
[*ludunt*] now' (979–80).[41] In pronouncing the cessation of the cult,
Myrrhina effectively is made to speak with the authority of the
Roman Senate. In this way she turns Lysidamus's attempt to divert
responsibility for his current distress to the female worshippers on its
head. The absurdity of the old man's claim only draws sharper focus
on his own Bacchic behaviour: it is now abundantly clear that
Lysidamus's utter lack of self-control and his sexual impulses, as well
as his disruption of family life in his frenzied and monomaniacal
pursuit of Casina, are solely responsible for his shameful predicament.
The only character suffering temporary insanity in *Casina* is the
lovesick Lysidamus, whose abrogation of reason and (for Roman
moralists) age- and gender-appropriate behaviour have now rendered
him a nearly naked comic dupe. Furthermore, the audience has just
learned of Lysidamus's involvement in a violent, quasi-sexual struggle
with another man, the bride Chalinus.[42] Lysidamus in fact embodies
virtually all the stereotypes associated with the Bacchic cultists.
This brief exchange between Lysidamus and Myrrhina is thus not
only a brilliantly ironic touch, but perhaps carries satirical import
in its pointed reversal of traditional gender roles (see pp. 87–92). In
the *paterfamilias*'s comic display of phallic madness raging out of
control, one might even see satire of male hysteria regarding the cult
of Bacchus.

Casina in Performance

Casina is a dazzling comedy of an ingenious playwright seemingly at his creative zenith. Twenty-three scenes of continuous action show-casing Plautus's musical virtuosity, linguistic dexterity and mastery of his comic genre are preceded by a long prologue that teasingly tells us little about the play to come and is followed by a short epilogue overloaded with what did not transpire in *Casina*. Plautus's sex farce features memorable stage spectacles, including an intensely com-petitive lottery scene, a delightfully subversive wedding ceremony and the female characters' masterful theatrical triumph in the closing scenes. *Casina* also makes unusual demands on spectators to imagine events taking place – or not actually taking place – offstage. These include Olympio's and Lysidamus's humiliating confessions about their 'honeymoon' with the bride Chalinus, and Pardalisca's virtuoso narrative of a fictive Casina raging inside Lysidamus's house.

Something fresh (prologue)

Casina features an impersonal prologue speaker,[1] probably an actor in the troupe who appears in costume, though unmasked.[2] After walking out and taking a position on the street in front of two houses represented on the stage's backdrop,[3] he speaks directly to the audience in musically unaccompanied iambics, the metre closest to everyday speech and standard in prologues. Behind him are the households of Lysidamus, identified simply as *senex* ('an old man', 35) and his neighbour Alcesimus, who is not named until his entrance (515).[4]

While the nominal setting is Athens, the prologue speaker's flattering designation of spectators as devotees of *Fides* (1–2), the Roman personification of Trust, indicates that the play's target audience and world are Roman.[5] We lack production information for *Casina*, but it is possible that the temporary theatre on this occasion was constructed before Fides' temple on the Capitoline Hill, near the city's pivotal temple of Jupiter Optimus Maximus and overlooking the Roman forum directly below. After perhaps gesturing to this grand venue, the prologue speaker asks spectators to applaud their mutually respectful relationship with Fides (3), which he melds with a wish that they will be 'fair-minded' (4) toward himself and so also the play.

The manuscript tradition then preserves lines (5–20) belonging to a revival performance of *Casina* sometime after Plautus's death (see p. 102). When the Plautine version of the prologue resumes, a stock joke about bankers in the Roman forum, closed for business during the current holiday (23–8), further reminds spectators that the Athenian comedy to follow is bound up with their own world; the prologue speaker's point could be visually enhanced by the proximity of the forum lying just below the Capitoline Hill. The emphasis on 'games' (*ludi … ludus* (25), *ludis* (27), *ludos* (28)) both underscores the festive, public occasion and augurs the theatrical games to come in *Casina*, above all its play-within-the-play.[6] The prologue speaker's broader aim lies in enticing spectators to enjoy the performance, as their receptivity to *Casina* and its comic world demands some disengagement from everyday concerns: 'let no one fear his creditor' (24).[7]

In the case of highly stereotyped New Comedy, experienced theatregoers probably sought assurances that they were about to see something 'new', that is, some variation on the genre's largely formulaic plots and characters. The prologue speaker provides the title – *Klēroumenoi* (31) in Greek, *The Lot-drawers* or *Sortientes* (32) in Latin[8] – of the source play by Diphilus and insists that Plautus has 'written it anew in Latin' (33–4). As he lays out the background to the plot (35–66), the prologue speaker drops several hints as to what exactly is fresh about *Casina*. The households, to which he frequently gestures (for example 'a married old man lives *here*', 35), are typically comic ones, consisting of married couples, their (legitimate) children and slaves. Similarly unremarkable is the prospect of the sixteen-year-old slave (39) who gives her name to the play being the object of an amorous struggle between father and son:[9] 'each now is lining up his troops against the other' (50). Spectators know that the elderly lover (*senex amator*) in such cases is by comic convention destined to lose the battle in his age-inappropriate pursuit. Casina, however, is not really a slave (as the audience soon learns, 81–2), but the freeborn daughter of the neighbours (revealed only in *Casina*'s epilogue), and so Lysidamus's plan to sexually exploit her can be viewed as illicit. The prologue speaker starts to reveal this important fact by introducing into his narrative the slave of Lysidamus who took the baby Casina from the woman exposing her sixteen years before and convinced his master's wife to raise the child (37–44). While the slave would play a critical role in a comedy – as probably in Diphilus's – featuring a scene in which the girl's free identity and eligibility for marriage were established onstage, the prologue speaker playfully claims that the slave is 'sick in bed' (37–8) and so unavailable to appear in *Casina*. The prologue speaker is intimating that one of Plautus's significant innovations is his jettisoning of a recognition scene (and perhaps a wedding) from his play and the relegation of this material to the play's epilogue (1012–18). The audience is given additional assurances that the girl has been raised as if she were freeborn, and so remains a virgin (45–6).

The primary novelty of *Casina*, however, lies in Plautus's shifting the father–son rivalry to husband (Lysidamus) and wife (Cleostrata, 'Glory of the army', named at 393). The son, Euthynicus ('Direct-victory', named in the epilogue, 1014), who presumably appeared in Diphilus, is altogether removed from *Casina*. The prologue speaker naturalistically explains his being sent abroad as motivated by Lysidamus's wish to eliminate his rival for Casina (60-2).[10] The prologue speaker informs the audience that Euthynicus will not return (as sons sent away on business by their fathers typically do in comedy) because he has been written out of Plautus's Latin translation: 'Plautus wrecked a bridge along the young man's way home' (65-6).[11] Had the son returned to compete with his father, *Casina* would have been a more conventional play (cf. *As., Merc.*). The metaphor of bridge-demolition isolates Plautus's creative choice in constructing a different comedy: the battle for control of Casina's body will instead foreground the complex politics of a Roman marriage. This loss in translation creates a refreshing contest between the couple that is fought through surrogates: Lysidamus will vie for Casina ('Cinnamon-Girl', named at 96) through his farm-manager (52-4), Olympio,[12] and Cleostrata, who somehow has ferreted out her husband's desires (58), will promote a marriage with her son's military attendant (55-7), the city slave Chalinus ('Horse-Bridle', first named at 104). We are never explicitly told that Cleostrata knows all along that Casina is the neighbours' freeborn child, but spectators might reasonably suspect this, given New Comedy convention and the manner in which Cleostrata is said to have raised the child, as well as the extent of her current efforts to preserve the girl for her son.

Marriage between slaves was not a legal possibility,[13] which the prologue speaker acknowledges as part of a playful rhetorical strategy to induce spectators into accepting the marriage by proxy plot:

> *What the . . .?* A slave wedding? Impossible!
> Since when do slaves propose or get married?
> It's unprecedented! It doesn't happen anywhere in the world!
>
>   68-70

The prologue speaker offers dubious precedents for such marriages among Carthaginians, Greeks and (Hellenized) Apulians (71-8), that is, 'Others' often stereotyped by Romans as perfidious (the 'enemies' of Fides herself), and in this way he exploits Roman comedy's Greek setting for his present advantage. That the prologue speaker is aware of the legal absurdity of his claim (for either a Greek or Roman audience) is made clear by his self-contradictory challenge to sceptical spectators to bet a jug of honeyed wine that he is lying, as long as the arbiter of the wager hails from one of these three (corruptible) peoples (75–7). The prologue speaker is coaxing spectators to suspend their disbelief about such marriages for the duration of *Casina*. Although spectators do not know exactly what sort of marriage actually lies ahead,[14] the prologue speaker is preparing them for the parodic marriage between the male slaves: they are being asked to make an imaginative leap that subverts traditional marriage.[15] The full extent of the prologue speaker's subterfuge here is only revealed in the play's faux wedding ceremony, with its disguise, costuming and role-playing.[16]

Further reassuring words about Casina conclude the prologue (79–86). Most importantly, she will prove to be a freeborn Athenian virgin eligible for marriage. As a free person, she will be untainted by illicit sexuality (82) in this comedy,[17] although the audience does not yet know that this is the case because she does not appear as a character in the play. One of the chief pleasures of *Casina* lies in the titular character's remaining an alluringly aromatic but unattainable object of desire for the male characters, whose physicality is entirely a construction of their sex-starved imaginations, a process in which spectators are also implicated (see pp. 89–91). The prologue speaker deceives spectators into assuming that Casina will appear onstage by joking that after the play male audience members can hire the actor who played her for a faux marriage (86), as Roman actors might of necessity prostitute themselves in real life.[18] The prologue speaker's joke thus highlights the grimmer aspects of the actors' everyday status, as also the sexual brutality a female slave like Casina was likely to endure (see pp. 81–7). The prologue speaker here also covertly presages the scene in which the all-too-male Chalinus will costume himself as a female bride in Cleostrata's plot (see pp. 65–70). The faux Casina (i.e. Chalinus) in the play is a male actor like the troupe member who might have played Casina and now is said to be available for lewd, 'nuptial' role-play after the play. As is conventional in Plautine prologues, this one ends swiftly with a flattering valediction to the citizen-soldiers in the audience (87–8). The prologue speaker exits and the stage is emptied for the start of the farce that spectators eagerly await.

Diversionary tactics (Scene 1)

Two slaves enter from Lysidamus's house in heated argument, with Chalinus closely tracking (92) Olympio's movement across the stage.[19] We unfortunately do not know if their masks and costumes, or the use of any props (for example a farm implement held by Olympio) visually distinguished city from country slave. Their banter soon enough identifies each character and his interests, although the conventional opposition between rusticity and urbanity it suggests proves to be a smokescreen.[20] The initially confident Chalinus predictably scorns the farm-manager as a manure-bred (114) creature out of his element (104), but Olympio never responds in kind with expected assaults on his urban counterpart's morality or masculinity. Olympio in fact begins to assume the upper hand over his interlocutor with his cheeky response to Chalinus about why he is 'crawling' about the city: 'I feel like it' (99).[21] Chalinus reasserts his superior (city) status and urges Olympio to return home (99–103), but Olympio in his response suggests that he is the more sophisticated of the pair by staking a claim to Casina in the urbane language of love ('the lovely and tender little Casina', 108).[22] Chalinus is impressed by Olympio's confident visualization of Casina as his bride in the country (104–11), and manages only a weak retort, 'You'll marry her? I'll hang myself before she's yours' (111–12). This pattern develops for the rest of the scene as Olympio articulates the various tortures he imagines Chalinus undergoing, first as an attendant at his wedding and then as his underling on the farm (117–31), where Chalinus's excruciating days will be capped by nights in which he is forced to observe the newlyweds' lovemaking (132–40). Olympio's expansive ideation is interrupted only by the defensive Chalinus's line, 'what'll you do?' (132). At the conclusion of his visionary harangue, Olympio pre-empts any response from Chalinus by rushing off toward his master's house; Chalinus gives chase ('I'm following you', 142), thereby concluding the scene precisely as it began.

Olympio thoroughly dominates the scene through his mastery of language and acting performance. He vividly details the toil and suffering ahead of Chalinus on the farm through metonymy ('one amphora … one path / … one spring … one bronze bucket … eight vats', 121–2) and metaphor ('you'll become a horse's crupper', 125; 'you'll eat dirt like an earthworm', 127), no doubt miming the actions he describes as the actor playing Chalinus makes cringing gestures. Olympio's coup de grace to the exhausted and famished Chalinus is his imaginary enactment of Casina's pillow talk. He impersonates Casina whispering amorous endearments into his ears ('my sweetheart, my Olympio, my life, my honeykins, my joy … my day of festival, my little love-bird,[23] my lovey-dovey, my bunny-rabbit', 134–8), which he sadistically imagines Chalinus witnessing while bound to their bedroom window. Chalinus in this way is reduced to the mouse trapped in a wall (140) Olympio envisions him to be, and, bested by the latter's imaginative flourish, can only meekly scurry after his tormentor to end the scene and empty the stage as they enter Lysidamus's house in succession (142–3). Given Olympio's commanding performance, especially his verbal dexterity, spectators at this point might expect him to assume the role of clever slave in the play. This prospect too proves to be illusory, as Olympio will launch no rebellious scheme to aid his (elderly) master's desire, and only passively participates in the proxy plot, while Lysidamus ultimately will be exposed as a 'true slave' (see pp. 73–6). The slaves ignore the proxy arrangement throughout the scene, as both assume the prospective marriage with Casina will be real (96, 102, 107, 109) and highlight the competition between each other rather than their masters.

The real battle (Scenes 2–4)

Casina is one of Plautus's most musical plays, as becomes evident in this rich tableaux of scenes introducing the female characters (Cleostrata, Pardalisca, Myrrhina) and Lysidamus. A lively series of songs (144–251) is crowned by the contentious exchange of husband and wife in musically accompanied trochaics (252–78), the most common metre in Plautus.[24] Cleostrata and her slave Pardalisca take the stage to deliver a brief opening song (144–64), a duet in which the latter has only a single line (her revelation that Lysidamus has demanded lunch, followed by her exit, 147).[25] Cleostrata opens in bacchiacs, a measure closely associated with women in Plautus,[26] and commences the 'exhalation' of the play's first musical arc (see p. 8 and Appendix). She instructs (unseen) slaves inside Lysidamus's house to keep the pantry locked while she visits her neighbour. Cleostrata's action suggests that she wields considerable power in the house,[27] and highlights the play's theme of food and sex: as she shortly notes, 'there'll be no cooking today' (149–50), since she plans to punish her philandering husband with hunger and thirst (152–6; see pp. 92–6). At this point in the play, spectators may mistakenly suppose that she is an unsympathetic 'stock comic shrew',[28] in Plautus a wife who uses the leverage afforded by her dowry to control her husband (see pp. 27–8). They of course have not yet met the ridiculous Lysidamus, at whom Cleostrata hurls a trifecta of epithets in her song: 'hell-fodder, chaser of disgrace, barnful of depravity' (159–61). Just as Cleostrata indicates her intention to 'complain about her situation' (162) to Myrrhina, ideally inside the latter's house, the doors of the neighbour's house creak and Myrrhina emerges. Before engaging Myrrhina, Cleostrata wonders about the timing (164), as the two women must now discuss a private matter on the street before their houses, as is the case for all conversations in Roman comedy.

The thematically pivotal **Scene 3** begins with Myrrhina,[29] properly accompanied out of doors by female slaves, instructing her slaves inside to notify her husband of her visit (165–7). She wears the same costume and mask as Cleostrata, but her request for a prop, a distaff (170–1), along with her admission that she is exhausted from her weaving and seeks her neighbour's company while working (168–9), signify that she is a very traditional *matrona*. The women's extended greeting (170–83) as they approach from opposite sides of the stage (for example Cleost. 'I was just coming to see you.' Myrrh. 'And I was doing the same to you', 178) suggests their reciprocal, choreographed movements onstage.[30]

The pair's intimacy is quickly established when Myrrhina sympathetically acknowledges her neighbour's dour expression (172–3).[31] After further warm greetings (179–84) and some evasive remarks about marital strife (185–92), Cleostrata divulges that her husband's desire for Casina and plan to give her to Olympio are the cause of her consternation (193–5a). Shocked at her friend's very public revelation, Myrrhina urges Cleostrata to be quiet, and Cleostrata assures her that they are alone (197–8).[32] In this way the women secure the audience's full attention and mark their conversation as especially important. When Myrrhina questions Cleostrata's claim that Casina is her concern and property, they in effect debate the rights of women within Roman marriage:

Myrrhina

> . . . But how is it she's yours?
> A decent wife's not supposed to have private property
> Behind her husband's back. If she does, it's damaged goods –
> You know, stolen from her husband or earned on her back!
>> In my opinion, all that's yours is your husband's.

Cleostrata

> You're disagreeing with your best friend about this?

Myrrhina

>> Shh,
> Silly person, and listen up:
> Don't oppose your husband.
> Let him lech, let him do whatever he wants, so long as he provides
>> for you at home.

Cleostrata

> Are you out of your mind? You're acting against your own interests.

Myrrhina

> No, silly!
> The one thing you never want to hear your husband say is –

Cleostrata

> What?

Myrrhina

> 'Out of the house, woman!'

198–212

Myrrhina here assumes a traditionalist stance by advocating the older form of Roman marriage (*cum manu*) whereby a father transferred his absolute power over his daughter to her husband (see pp. 25–7). Cleostrata is made to favour a more 'modern' marriage arrangement (*sine manu*), one in which fathers retained their power over married daughters, who might keep property separate from their husbands. The prospect of hearing the phrase 'Out of the house, woman!' (212), a Roman formula of divorce,[33] seems to exert far less influence over Cleostrata than Myrrhina, and perhaps explains why she is less tolerant than her neighbour of her husband's lechery. Their debate abruptly ends at this point when Cleostrata notes the approach of Lysidamus and urges her neighbour to be quiet and go back inside her house (213–14). As the women say goodbye, they agree to resume their conversation (215–16), though this never takes place onstage.[34] Cleostrata does not state her plan to eavesdrop at the scene's end, but nonetheless takes up a suitable position for this onstage, as she will go unnoticed by Lysidamus until 228.

In **Scene 4**, Lysidamus, returning from the forum, exuberantly bursts onto the stage, completely ignorant of his own ridiculousness and his wife's surveillance.[35] His solo song's subject is love itself, the finest spice of all, which he believes can transform even a grumpy old man into someone 'charming and chill' (223). His grotesque appearance as a grimly masked, white-haired and bearded comic *senex* visually belies this claim. Moreover, the geriatric singer's padded costume is dishevelled, as we soon learn when Cleostrata accuses him of patronizing a brothel and being intoxicated (242–6). Most ludicrous of all is Lysidamus's confident application of this maxim about love's force as a condiment to his own condition: 'Now that I'm in love with Casina, I've become the spitting image of Spiffiness herself' (225). His purchase of every charming cologne (226) in town, Lysidamus believes, has magically made him irresistible: '[I'm perfumed] to please her, and I think I do please her. But my wife's every breath is torture' (227). Far from a (young) lover exuding a pleasant scent to match Casina's, we imagine only an old man reeking of competing colognes and stale alcohol; in keeping with the elite moral tradition of Rome, an actor might play Lysidamus as decadently effeminate.[36] And all his self-assured effusiveness is undermined by the fact that his wife is absorbing his every word.

Lysidamus is brought down to earth some by the sudden sight of his wife's grim expression. In an overly confident aside the old man announces his plan to charm Cleostrata. Lysidamus's alliteratively saccharine address of her as his 'dear wife and source of delight' (229),

no doubt accompanied by cajoling gestures, is sharply rebuffed: 'Get
away and get your hands off me!' (229a). Designating Cleostrata 'his
Juno' (that is, to his philandering Jove!), his attempt to physically
assuage her provokes a similar reaction: 'Let go of me!' (231). Their
duet becomes an onstage chase (231–1a), as Cleostrata eludes
Lysidamus's inept groping until she stops and asks him if he is sane.
Unassuaged by his claim of being 'sanely in love' (232) with her,
Cleostrata expresses her preference for a soberer connubial relationship (233). When she notes that his unwanted passion is 'killing her',
the bumbling *senex* commiserates with the audience in an aside by
wishing this were literally true (234). The ever-vigilant *matrona*, as an
index of her growing theatrical power, overhears the aside and turns
her back to him in disgust (cf. 235). Cleostrata faces him again to
confront him about the tell-tale cologne she perhaps pretends only
now to catch scent of (236). This time Lysidamus's aside about being
caught red-handed goes unnoticed by his wife, but his vigorous efforts
to wipe off his scented hair-gels with his cloak (237) confirm her
charge and make him look utterly foolish. Cleostrata encapsulates
Lysidamus's shamefully age-inappropriate behaviour: 'you worthless
old man, promenading through town and reeking of cologne!' (240).
Unpersuaded by Lysidamus's claim that he was helping a friend
purchase cologne (241), Cleostrata points to his wrinkled cloak as
evidence that he has been in a brothel, adding that such behaviour
jeopardizes his wealth (248) as well as his reputation.[37] Cleostrata
cannot be readily dismissed as a stereotypically nagging wife here, as
her views align closely with conservative Roman moral tradition in
identifying the potential threat her husband's behaviour poses to their
household finances – and she seems theatrically in charge of the
scene.

A richly ironic exchange between the spouses concludes the scene.
Unable to mount a plausible defence to Cleostrata's charges, Lysidamus
reasserts his authority as *paterfamilias* and, resorting to gender

stereotypes, urges Cleostrata to regain control of her emotions (!) and oblige her husband (249–53). He firmly states his wish to have Casina married to Olympio and asserts that the farm-manager will make a better provider than Chalinus (254–8). Undaunted, Cleostrata accuses him of age-inappropriate dereliction of duty, as evidenced by his inordinate interest in the affairs of the household's female slaves (259–61). While Cleostrata, as *materfamilias*, might reasonably lay claim to supervision of the female slaves, spectators are aware of her special concern for Casina since taking her in as an exposed infant – the spouses' exchange has become increasingly tense. As Lysidamus's attempts to persuade his wife of his omnipotence in the household founder (263–5), she warns that he's 'asking for trouble' (266). Lysidamus in an aside suspects that his wife has 'gotten wind' of his intentions (266), and she ironically asks, 'why are you so desperately desirous of that match of yours?' (267). Having now reached an impasse, the couple agree to allow each other to attempt to persuade the other's surrogate to relinquish his claim to Casina. Lysidamus is left alone onstage to curse his wife for her resistance, but his monologue wins him no sympathy. The *senex* inaptly portrays himself as one of Roman comedy's feckless *young* men in love: 'Poor me! I'm utterly tortured by love' (276). When Lysidamus reiterates his fear that Cleostrata has 'gotten wind' (277; cf. 266) of his plan, the verb of smelling, far from eliciting sympathy, only diverts attention to the old man's stench.

Impotent mastery (Scenes 5–6)

As **Scene 4** ends, Lysidamus's thoughts turn to his wife's support for Chalinus (278). No sooner does Lysidamus curse Chalinus than the slave appears and is about to disrespectfully say, 'your wife said that you should be cursed', before instead completing his sentence, 'that you were calling me' (279–80). Cleostrata, who we are to imagine is simultaneously making a pitch to Olympio inside, has sent Chalinus out. In **Scene 5** we witness Lysidamus's inability to persuade Chalinus to give up his pursuit of Casina, while in **Scene 6**, when Olympio reports Cleostrata's failure to prevail upon him, our suspicions that Lysidamus fears his wife and seems incapable of bending her to his will are confirmed. The social actualities of a Roman household no doubt were more complex than a *paterfamilias*'s theoretically absolute power over both its free and enslaved members might lead us to believe, a reality that comedy exploits (see p. 24). Lysidamus in **Scenes 5–6** is shown to be utterly not in control of his *familia*. The *senex* is remarkably inept in his dealings with household subordinates, as we see most clearly in his exchange with Chalinus. Upon entering, Chalinus curtly orders his master to reveal the reason for calling him outside (280). Lysidamus at first chastises Chalinus for his disrespect, ordering him to change his sour expression (281–2), but soon resorts to flattering his slave: 'I've long considered you a decent and honest fellow' (283). Chalinus proposes his own manumission in light of his master's high opinion of himself. The old man then unsuccessfully attempts to bribe Chalinus with the promise of freedom for his compliance regarding Casina (284–92). When Chalinus remains obstinate, Lysidamus relents and sends him inside to fetch the necessary equipment for the lottery to decide Casina's fate, irrationally declaring that he'll take his revenge via the lots as he in reality surrenders to chance (298–9). As the unperturbed Chalinus exits, he forecasts his victory, and Lysidamus is left to deliver a monologue declaring his helplessness: 'Am I not a wretched fellow? Surely, the whole world's lined up against me' (304). Having failed to exercise any authority over his wife and slave, Lysidamus declares himself destined to become a 'non-existent old man' (305), in effect 'dead'. With all his hopes now tied to the lottery for Casina, Lysidamus imagines, in defeat, the prospect of suicide in the manner of Ajax: 'I'll make my sword a mattress and lie on it' (307–8).[38] This homely comic phrase undermines any seriousness here and mention of a sword initiates what becomes a running phallic metaphor. Lysidamus's melodramatic musings are interrupted by Olympio's entrance from the house (309). As the play's first musical arc (1–308) concludes, Lysidamus has again failed to win the sympathy he craves from spectators.

As the music (playing since 144) stops, Olympio appears, shouting back to Cleostrata inside that not even torture in an oven could deter him from pursuing Casina (309–11). Both Lysidamus and Cleostrata have failed to persuade each other's proxy, and so the lottery scene is definitely on. Lysidamus is revived by Olympio's determination. Master and slave exchange misogynistic and sexual jests at Cleostrata's expense, thus continuing to promote the ill-conceived narrative that she is merely a shrew. Olympio reports having gone so far as to aver that he would not yield to Jupiter in the matter of Casina (323–4),[39] for which he claims the entire household has now declared him its enemy (329–30). Lysidamus's insistence that he is Jupiter, and so the only domestic power to be venerated, does not appease Olympio, who draws attention to the local (i.e. elderly) Jupiter's mortality and the likely succession of lesser deities in the household (330–7). The slave comes off as smarter than his deluded master here. Lysidamus ignores Olympio's concerns with vivid thoughts of sex with Casina (339), to which Olympio notes the determined resistance of Juno-Cleostrata (340–1). Rapt in his erotic fantasy, Lysidamus mutters semi-coherently about the lottery (342–4). To Olympio's fear that the lottery may work against them, Lysidamus urges words of good omen and trust in the gods (345–6). Olympio questions the prudence of his master's pious fidelity, but further theological discussion is squelched by Lysidamus's acknowledgement of Chalinus's approach with the urn (351–2). Cleostrata follows closely behind him. The *senex* grandly heralds the contest at hand: 'It's time for us to fight it out in pitched battle' (352).[40]

A chancy spectacle (Scenes 7–8)

The musical accompaniment starts up again for this emotionally intense scene, the first in *Casina* to feature at least four speakers (cf. Scenes 19, 21, 23).[41] Chalinus eventually places the urn down somewhere near centre stage (363), so that it remains a focal point throughout the scene,[42] and the pairs of aligned characters face off around it, always leaving the audience's view of the urn unobscured.[43] The urn contains water (385) and Chalinus has brought two counters of submergible, but indissoluble material for the lottery. The counters, which Chalinus handed to Lysidamus earlier (363), are distributed to each side by Lysidamus (374–9). Fearing trickery, Chalinus inspects the urn for additional counters (379–80). Cleostrata perhaps stands closest to the urn once it is set onstage, and clearly does so when Lysidamus orders her to shake it and the counters inside.[44]

Despite all this anticipatory excitement onstage, the harsh fact remains that sexual control of Casina's body is at stake in the lottery.[45] Individual spectators may have a favourite horse in this race, for a host of subjective reasons. The audience knows that, while Olympio has expressed a wish to marry his fellow slave, the grotesque Lysidamus only intends to sexually violate her. On the other side, Chalinus's aims match Olympio's,[46] although the prologue planted hints that a better outcome for a free Casina may lie ahead (see p. 39). Casina's ultimate fate, however, apart from the assurance that she will suffer no sexual violation in the play (82–3), remains uncertain, and so there is genuine tension surrounding the lot-drawing, which in Roman life was a solemn, ritual occasion, and here is assumed to be in the gods' hands (346–9).[47] Regular theatregoers probably suspect that 'team-Lysidamus' is destined to win the lottery, so that the comic plot may further evolve. They will also expect any victory by the *senex* to be temporary, as comic convention demands youth's triumph over age in love. Spectators could not at this point predict what Cleostrata has in store for her lecherous husband.

Olympio and Chalinus, in a familiar Plautine slave-shtick, threaten each other throughout the lottery scene in creatively violent, metaphorical language.[48] Chalinus declares himself 'a cattle-prod digging at [Olympio's] heart' (361–2). Chalinus completes Olympio's prayer for success for him: 'that you win a dog's chain and a yoke of torture today' (389). He further hopes that the lots bring hanging and the prospect of 'blowing your eyes out through your nose' (391). Olympio counters with a jest about Chalinus's compliance in his own rape (362) and a wish that Chalinus's body liquefy from the heat generated by whipping (400).[49] For citing the learned mythical exemplum of the Heraclidae (the sons of Hercules), Olympio deems his rival 'a man of letters' (*litteratus*, 401), an allusion to the branding of fugitive slaves. Any distinctions between country and city slave are largely elided in the scene. The farm-manager is given an urbane jest when he ascribes his victory in the lottery to his own *pietas* and that of his ancestors (418; see pp. 20–1). All this verbal violence is instantiated when, just before the lot is drawn, Lysidamus orders Olympio to strike Chalinus in the face (404), and Cleostrata has Chalinus respond in kind (407): 'Husband and wife pummel each other by proxy.'[50] In their post-fight analysis, Olympio and Chalinus justify the violence as prescribed by Jupiter and Juno, respectively (407–8). The scene thus in most concrete, visual terms renews the idea of *Casina* as an Olympian power struggle between the couple – and hints at a revenge plot by 'Juno'.

Though Lysidamus attempts to appear dignified, as if a calm, disinterested observer and *paterfamilias* (375–7), his lust and lack of self-control are highlighted in the first of several Freudian slips,[51] when he makes a last desperate effort to avert the lottery: 'I was thinking, my dear wife, that I'd prevail upon you to let Casina marry me' (364–5). Cleostrata points out his mistake, but the old man's gargantuan desires again cause him to confuse pronouns (366–7). Lysidamus's attempt to explain all as mere linguistic blundering elicits a sharp rejoinder from Cleostrata about his behaviour. Oblivious to her pointed irony, Lysidamus only digs himself a deeper hole by ironically replying, 'That's what happens when you really want something a lot' (370). Lysidamus's repeated mistakes show just how poorly equipped he is to pull off a scheme: he is a miserable actor in that he cannot sustain a convincing role.[52] As Cleostrata reaches into the urn, Lysidamus in an aside reveals that he is suffering heart palpitations (414–15),[53] no doubt visually expressed by the actor playing him. Cleostrata by contrast remains composed throughout the scene, in which she significantly speaks less frequently than the men. She quietly presides over the lottery with dignity – Lysidamus asks her to draw the lot at 394, but she is delayed by the slaves' antics until 415 – and her stage presence here may again recall that of Lysistrata in the finale of Aristophanes' play. Cleostrata calmly announces the outcome to Chalinus as she shows Lysidamus his winning lot, and he inappropriately exclaims, 'it's mine' (416).[54] The patriarch's confidence restored, Lysidamus orders his wife to make preparations for the wedding (417–19), not without gloating (421), and hints at a plan to escort the newlyweds to the country (420; cf. 477–87). Cleostrata utters a single word of agreement and exits into the house, and, as is confirmed when she returns in **Scene 11**, now fully cognizant of her husband's plans and preparing to exact her revenge. Lysidamus leads Olympio inside, in what will prove to be a vain effort to accelerate the wedding preparations, thus leaving Chalinus alone onstage. Before exiting into the house, Lysidamus pointedly tells Olympio that Chalinus is not to be trusted (423). In the short monologue that follows,[55] Chalinus hints that he has new comic ambitions. After expressing regret over the loss of Casina, Chalinus reveals his suspicions about the old man's inappropriate behaviour during the lottery (429–33). The creaking of doors, a stock New Comedy device to signal an entrance,[56] alerts Chalinus to the entrance of Olympio and his master; employing a military metaphor (of ambush, 436), Chalinus positions himself to seize the opportunity for eavesdropping.

Ravenous ambitions (Scenes 9–10)

The co-conspirators – Olympio decked out in bridegroom's white (446), Lysidamus clutching a bag of coins for provisions (490) – enter in spirited conversation and, as if to make Chalinus's ears burn, speculate as to how they might further rub defeat in his face (437–43). Chalinus signposts his own movement: 'I'll withdraw to the wall like a scorpion' (443), indicating that he will sidle up to the backdrop behind the actors.[57] From this position he communicates with spectators in his asides, thus splitting the audience's focus between himself and Lysidamus and Olympio. As an internal audience during the scene, Chalinus mocks Lysidamus's inhuman lust, as he also intercepts the old man's plan and suggests to the audience that Lysidamus is now doomed to failure.[58] Unaffected by the pair's *Schadenfreude*, Chalinus resolves to postpone his own suicide so that he can see Olympio meet his demise first (447–8).

As Olympio celebrates his role in the sham-marriage to provide his master sexual access to Casina behind his wife's back, the fearful *senex* orders him to keep quiet (451) but cannot contain his own joy at the plan's success and moves toward Olympio as if to kiss him, addressing the farm-manager as his 'darling' (453). In keeping with Plautus's preference for vivid sexual euphemism, Chalinus in an aside comments, 'I do believe he intends to burrow into the bailiff's bladder' (455).[59] Lysidamus's homoeroticism toward Olympio only accelerates, and he slips behind his slave and mock-sexually mounts him from behind (456–9). Suggesting that Lysidamus's sexual aggression may be habitual rather than a symptom of his current infatuation, Chalinus speculates that Olympio acquired his bailiff's post through sexual

acquiescence and relates Lysidamus's similar attempt to make himself
a 'butler/back-doorman' (460–2; see pp. 85–6). Chalinus's eavesdropping thus enhances the audience's sense of the old man's
monstrous libido. Chalinus's prediction that the two 'will join feet
today' (465)[60] also anticipates Lysidamus's forthcoming moves to
mount his slave like a stallion (**Scene 19**), as well as his sexual
surrender to Olympio (**Scene 15**).

Aroused by his amorous frolicking with Olympio, Lysidamus
throws all caution to the wind and exclaims, 'Oh the kisses I'll plant on
Casina today! So many delights to be had behind my wife's back!'
(467–8). Chalinus gains confirmation of his suspicions and is
reinvigorated and borrows a phrase from Plautus's clever slaves: 'I've
got these guys' (470). Lysidamus continues fantasizing about Casina:
'I'm champing at the bit to hug and kiss her' (471). Lysidamus divulges
his plan to make the assignation with Casina immediately possible:
Alcesimus is to send his wife to help Cleostrata and spend the night
with her, thus leaving the neighbours' house available for a 'honeymoon'
with Casina (486). In the plan's conceit, Alcesimus's house represents
'the country', that is, Lysidamus's country estate, to where Olympio
ostensibly is to escort his bride, accompanied by Lysidamus. The old
man makes this clear for spectators by pointing to the house on the
stage backdrop (485). Overflowing with confidence and self-
congratulations, the *senex* revels in what he imagines to be his
unassailable cleverness. Chalinus, however, suggests in his aside that
another plot awaits the pair: 'Keep on plotting away: your cleverness
only puts your life in great peril' (488–9). Still deluded about his
urbanity, the aged lover thinks of foodstuffs for the wedding and
hands the wallet he holds to Olympio with these instructions: 'I do
want things to go elegantly – hurry off now and get delicacies fit for a
girl so delicate' (492–3). Lysidamus's request for sole inspires a pun
by Chalinus about smashing the old man's face with an entire shoe
(495–6), which ironically suggests Lysidamus is setting himself up for

violent punishment. Olympio exits for the market while Lysidamus goes to Alcesimus's house to confirm their conspiracy. Chalinus, left alone onstage, jubilantly steps forwards to address the audience.

In a monologue that continues the rapport with the audience he has built through his asides,[61] Chalinus declares that he would not trade the price of his freedom (three times over) to forgo informing to his mistress and exacting revenge from the pair (504–6). Chalinus thus is made to sound like one of Plautus's clever slaves, a subordinate who schemes for his master even when this works against his own self-interest and holds no prospect of manumission. Chalinus will launch no scheme beyond informing to Cleostrata. Plautus is subtly preparing us for Cleostrata's appropriation of the role of a clever slave (see pp. 57, 70, 97–8). Chalinus declares victory for the defeated and employing a metaphor that is programmatic for deception in Plautine comedy[62] pledges to 'cook up' a plot distinctly different from the old man's (511–14). Riffing on Lysidamus's recent order for foodstuffs to celebrate the planned nuptials, Chalinus delivers a tongue-twister on the comic fare he will see is prepared (511–14), where the extended cooking metaphor mockingly recalls Lysidamus's opening song (**Scene 4**) about love as the spice of life. At roughly the mid-point of *Casina*, spectators can be confident that Chalinus and Cleostrata will frustrate Lysidamus, though their precise means to accomplish this is uncertain. With Chalinus's exit into Lysidamus's house (he will not be seen again until he emerges as the bride Casina, 814), the stage is briefly empty, which promotes an illusion that time has passed when Lysidamus and Alcesimus enter at 515, though this is not necessarily a high priority in Plautine comedy.[63]

The old men emerge from Alcesimus's house in mid-conversation. Lysidamus asks Alcesimus to spare him moralizing criticism of his age-inappropriate philandering, thereby rhetorically emphasizing what he does not want to hear (517–19).[64] Lysidamus entirely misses the import of his neighbour's remark, 'I've never seen anyone more wretched (520) from love than you', which metacomically identifies Lysidamus as a poor specimen of a (young) comic lover. Lysidamus nonetheless has secured his neighbour's complicity, and Alcesimus agrees to send his slaves together with his wife to Cleostrata, so that his house may be emptied for Lysidamus's sex-plot (521–2). Lysidamus remains deaf to his neighbour's wise admonition about being too clever for his own good and boldly declares, 'What's the point of being in love if you can't also be suave and sophisticated?' (529). The hubristic extent of the old man's fantasy in imagining himself to be an urbane young lover can be glimpsed through comparison with a similar claim by Calidorus in *Pseudolus*, one of Plautus's despondent young lovers: 'there's no fun if a lover doesn't behave foolishly' (*Ps.* 238). Comic convention places these two lovers on opposite trajectories: Calidorus necessarily 'gets the girl', while a much less pleasurable outcome awaits Lysidamus. Lysidamus enthusiastically sets off for the forum and Alcesimus returns to his house. The stage again is emptied of all characters until Cleostrata reappears for her brief monologue (531–8).

A change of course (Scenes 11–13)

In this triad of scenes, Cleostrata, now apprised of her husband's conspiracy,[65] actively commences her plot to punish Lysidamus. For now we see her acting alone, which clearly establishes her as the instigator of a plot to punish Lysidamus that eventually includes Pardalisca (**Scene 14**), Myrrhina (**Scene 20**) and the bride Chalinus. **Scene 11** commences when Cleostrata enters and reveals her knowledge of Lysidamus's plan to use Alcesimus's house for the assault on Casina. Plautus has his characters make competing pitches for rapport with spectators in separate entrance monologues here. Cleostrata enjoys the advantages of superior knowledge and of being able to sarcastically introduce her socially prominent neighbour as 'the pillar of the senate, the sentinel of the city' (536) immediately after divulging her intent to befuddle the conspiring 'castrated old rams' (535). Alcesimus expresses concern about Myrrhina's not yet having been summoned until he notices Cleostrata. He has no idea how overmatched he already is by Cleostrata's intelligence-gathering operation. She is also an accomplished actor, and politely and promptly convinces her neighbour that she needs no additional help at home (541–8).

After declining Alcesimus's offer of his wife's help with the wedding, Cleostrata bids the flummoxed old man farewell and moves away, as if to enter her house (548). Wrongly believing that he is alone onstage, Alcesimus delivers a desperate monologue ('What should I do now?', 549). Alcesimus now regrets his alliance with the 'worthless, toothless goat' (550) next door, which has induced him to degradingly offer his wife's services as 'a plate-licker' (552).[66] He suspects Cleostrata has gotten wind of the conspiracy, but concludes she knows nothing because she did not loudly remonstrate with him just now (554–6); Alcesimus, to his own detriment, assumes that Cleostrata is merely a comic shrew, and so incapable of assuming any other theatrical role. After he exits, Cleostrata steps forth from her eavesdropping position to declare success and draw attention to the old men's poor execution of their plot: 'the way those wretched old fools fret!' (558). She then appropriates the celebratory, metacomic language of Plautine clever slaves: 'how beautifully I've befuddled him' (*est lepide ludificatus*, 558), 'if only my husband were here for me to befuddle too' (*ludificem* ... *delusi*, 560).[67] As she announces her plan to set the pair of old men at loggerheads, she spots Lysidamus as he returns from the forum looking the part of, as Cleostrata ironically notes, a man of *grauitas* (562). His business in town apparently has forced the *senex* to assume an outward aura of respectability (and to sober up?), in sharp contrast to his earlier disorganized encounter with Cleostrata.

The music stops and Lysidamus, unaware of his wife's presence, confesses to spectators how his erotic distraction impeded him in the forum:

> What possibly could be stupider
> Than for a man in love to go to the forum
> On the very day what he love's available?
> That's how stupid I was when I squandered the day
> Helping a foolish relative of mine in court!
> It gives me great delight to say he lost his case:
> He got his just deserts for asking me to court today.

563–9

Rather than expressing shame or regret over his legal incompetence, Lysidamus chastises his relative's untimely request for assistance (570–3). The old man's infatuation has now tarnished his public reputation. Lysidamus suddenly notices Cleostrata standing in front of their house and fears (correctly) that she has overheard him (574–5).[68] Cleostrata affirms this in her aside and the two move closer together to speak. Lysidamus quickly turns to the pressing matter of vacating Alcesimus's house. To stir confusion, Cleostrata claims she followed Lysidamus's order but Alcesimus refused to send his wife (581–4). Lysidamus then rebukes his wife for not cajoling his friend (584), to which Cleostrata replies, 'coaxing other women's husbands is a prostitute's job, not a wife's, my dear' (585–6), suggesting that her husband is acting like a pimp: skilled actor that she is, she has delivered a perfect line here. She advises Lysidamus to fetch Myrrhina himself, and as she exits shares her delight at the forthcoming misunderstanding with the audience (598–90).

Before Lysidamus can knock on the neighbours' door, the slighted Alcesimus appears, and the old men exchange insults over the confusion wrought by Cleostrata (591–602). In a characteristic Plautine routine[69] their argument dissolves into an absurd linguistic contest to get in the last 'well' (*quin*), which is repeated eleven times over nine lines with ascending emphasis; Alcesimus 'wins' with 'well then, by Hercules, you can just go to hell!' (609). Alcesimus ultimately relents and agrees to send Myrrhina next door 'by way of the garden' (613), which will allow Myrrhina to emerge from Lysidamus's house in **Scene 20** without appearing onstage before then. As Alcesimus withdraws into his house, Lysidamus praises him ('you're a friend, a real bro', 615). Relieved but still discombobulated by this obstacle to his plan, Lysidamus, alone onstage, wonders if he has offended Venus. But before he can elaborate he suddenly hears a commotion ('What's that shouting?', 621) coming from inside his house. Cleostrata's revenge is now in full swing.

Woe to the conquerors (Scene 14)

Pardalisca ('Little Panther'),[70] Cleostrata's female slave-accomplice, bursts out of the house to launch an enthralling song (621–719).[71] Pardalisca's arresting opening in highly stylized language, featuring anaphora, alliteration, assonance and (unusually in Latin) rhyme, immediately evokes the world of tragedy:

> I'm done, I'm done, I'm utterly, utterly dead!
> Panic's paralyzed my heart, my languid limbs are trembling!
> I haven't a clue where to seek or search for
> Any sort of shelter, safety, or support!
> Such strange events in stranger ways I've seen
> Inside our house – boldness, brazenness not seen before!
>
> 621–6

To further seize Lysidamus's attention – and activate his fear – Pardalisca calls back to Cleostrata inside, imploring her mistress to seek protection and find a way to snatch the sword from 'that girl who has lost her mind' (629–9a), suggesting a Maenad is on a potentially murderous rampage. In an aside Lysidamus expresses shock at the report, no doubt initially shared by spectators, and addresses his slave directly ('*Pardalisca!*', 631) to commence a lively duet with much stage business. Pardalisca delivers a virtuoso performance as a distressed female character delivering a (in this case entirely fictional) messenger speech, a device widely used in ancient drama, especially tragedy, often to represent violence that would be difficult to stage. Pardalisca further signposts her entrance as (para-)tragic by responding to Lysidamus's call in the artificial diction of tragedy (as it was stereotyped in comedy): 'whence do these sounds take up residence in my ears?' (631).

Pardalisca begins her narrative with a summary declaration: 'I'm dead' (631), 'I'm dead, and you too have died' (633). The dazed Lysidamus makes a ready comic interlocutor here: 'What, you're dead? . . . Oh, I'm dead?' (633). As the scene unfolds he finds himself increasingly 'dead': 'I'm dead and buried' (665), 'I'm dead' (683), 'I'm the deadest man of all who are alive' (692). Pardalisca's speech is further delayed by Lysidamus's comic parroting of her exclamation, 'Woe to you': 'No, no, that should be "woe to you"' (634). Spectators may now suspect that things are not so dire as they first seemed. Without divulging details about the crisis inside, Pardalisca in mockery of her master instead plays a terrified and vulnerable woman in distress (634a–45). Pardalisca swoons in a sexualized manner and forces Lysidamus to fan her with his cloak while supporting her limp body (636–7).[72] Her seductive plea to 'take hold of [her] ears' (641), an invitation to kissing,[73] leads Lysidamus to realize that she may be mocking him. Assuming his master's role, he curses her, along with 'her breast, ears and head' (642), and threatens to beat her with his walking-stick (644). Since spectators still do not know that Casina will not appear in the play, some tension still surrounds the vague report of a sword-wielding female raging inside.

Slave and master address each other flirtatiously by their formal titles (*ere mi / mea . . . ancilla*, 646), and swap barbs ('You're too cruel'; 'You speak too soon', 647). Pardalisca resumes her narrative, though more verbal sparring follows as she only increases her master's curiosity and anxiety by obvious delay in what amounts to a verbal striptease (648–56).[74] Pardalisca even drops a clear hint that Casina is no slave when she asserts that the girl is behaving in a manner 'unbefitting of her Athenian upbringing' (652). The maid eventually blurts out that the sword-wielding Casina 'is imitating a bad example set by bad women by threatening to kill her husband' (657–8). Mention of 'bad women' behind Casina's actions ironically suggests Cleostrata and Myrrhina are devising a scheme after the fashion of Plautus's clever slaves, who openly revel in their 'badness'.[75] More delay and deceit follow, as Pardalisca dangles the keywords 'life' and 'sword' (658–9a) before her master. As a scene of tragic myth, the situation Pardalisca describes recalls the Danaids, who slay their husbands on their wedding night. The phallic sword prefigures the violent encounter between Chalinus-as-Casina and Lysidamus and his farm-manager (**Scenes 21–3**): '[she swore] she'll kill whoever sleeps with her tonight' (671). This last avowal triggers another Freudian slip from Lysidamus: 'She'll kill me?' (672). Pardalisca jettisons her tragic messenger's persona to incredulously ask Lysidamus, 'Just how does any of this pertain to you?' (672).[76] After ineptly explaining his mistake, the *senex* bluntly asks if Casina is threatening him (676). Seizing on Lysidamus's obvious fear, and as if improvising on the spot, Pardalisca insists that Casina is raging against the old man as the person responsible for her marriage: 'she says she won't allow your life, her own, or her husband's last until tomorrow' (678–9).

This animated exchange is then interrupted by a clever stroke of metacomedy, when Lysidamus proclaims to the audience, 'There isn't and never has been a *senex amator* as wretched as me' (684–5), where the old man's wretchedness refers to his performance as much as his state of mind. Pardalisca in turn congratulates herself for her fine performance and confirms in her aside that Cleostrata, and, surprisingly, Myrrhina are the directors behind her fictional account:

> I'm playing [*ludo*] him quite cleverly!
> Everything I just told him was complete fiction:
> My mistress and the neighbour lady here conceived this trick,
> And I was sent out to play [*ludere*] him!

> 685–8

Pardalisca's language explicitly indicates that the women have launched a trick worthy of a clever slave and her tragic performance here is part of a comedy at Lysidamus's expense. The frightened Lysidamus attempts to gather himself but struggles for words to ask if Casina still has the sword. Pardalisca, assuming the upper hand, shows impatience ('you're delaying me', 690) and perhaps begins to move toward the house. Playing off Lysidamus's fear, Pardalisca now claims Casina has two swords, one for each of her intended victims (692–3), which compels Lysidamus to declare himself 'the deadest man alive' and contemplate wearing a corselet that will cover his trunk and genitals (695).

Continuing his impotent style of mastery, Lysidamus suddenly thinks of Cleostrata and asserts it is her responsibility to dissuade Casina from violence. This, Pardalisca counters, is impossible unless plans for the marriage to Olympio are scrapped. Lysidamus attempts to reassert himself as Casina's master ('she'll get married today whether or not she consents to it', 700), but quickly undermines his resolution with yet another Freudian slip about marrying her himself (701–3). As the scene and song approach closure, the discombobulated *senex* asks his maid to beg his wife to entreat Casina again, so that he may safely enter his own house (704–6). Master and slave engage in one last ridiculous, mirrored exchange: Lys. 'And you must ask her.' Pard. 'I'll ask her.' Lys. 'But ask her nicely, in that special way of yours'

(707). Lysidamus is reduced to childishly negotiating with a subordinate. Pardalisca agrees to appeal to Cleostrata, but only after she secures various bribes (shoes, a gold ring, et al.) from Lysidamus (707–12). She again asserts her superior status by complaining that Lysidamus is delaying her (715–17). After her stunning performance, Pardalisca at last exits into the house just as the beleaguered Lysidamus, deprived of an opportunity for a monologue, spots Olympio returning from shopping with groceries and a 'procession' (719) of caterers.

Something's cooking alright (Scenes 15–17)

After a brief duet between Olympio and the cook Chytrio (cf. Greek *chytra*, 'pot')[77] that exploits the comic stereotype of hired cooks as thieves, the farm-manager, puffed up by the prospect of his wedding, spots Lysidamus and broadcasts his intention to swagger (as he no doubt exaggeratedly does onstage) before his master: 'Why don't I clothe myself in grand, aristocratic style?' (723–3a). Such self-aggrandizement on the part of clever slaves is not unusual in Plautus,[78] but as we have seen, Olympio is no schemer.[79] Plautus's usage of the verb *amicio*, 'clothe', elsewhere suggests[80] that it is to be taken literally here (rather than referring figuratively to a scheme), and so Olympio perhaps throws something over his slave's costume to suggest the longer, flowing garment of a free person or he mimics this action. All this preparation by Olympio to meet his master contributes to this scene's central theme: Lysidamus's degrading behaviour effectively has made him Olympio's slave.

Lysidamus needs little coaxing to assume his inverted role: he politely greets Olympio (724) and remarks on the farm-manager's newly acquired elegance ('quite a slick entrance there', 726). The old man suggestively edges up, but his foul breath repulses the farm-manager, who tries to move away. Lysidamus persists in rubbing up against Olympio (727–33), thus resuming his previous homoerotic aggression (**Scene 11**). During their cat and mouse chase across the stage (bounded as they are by Chtryio's surrounding team), Olympio, as a reflection of his (pretend) elite status, suddenly lapses into Greek sexual euphemism: 'You're really giving me a hard time here' (729).[81] Lysidamus threateningly counters in Greek: 'I'll give you a hard time, if you don't stand still' (729–30).[82] Following further attempts to avoid the feisty old man (and nearly vomiting, 733), Olympio arrogantly responds to Lysidamus's command ('Wait!', 734): 'What is it and who's asking me?' (734). Lysidamus feebly attempts to reassert his authority as master (735), but is rebuffed by the surly farm-manager: 'Aren't I a free person? Think again, think ...' (736–7). More horseplay ensues, and at Olympio's imperious command, 'Let go of me' (737), Lysidamus realizes that his sex-plot has made him dependent on Olympio and verbally surrenders: 'I'm your slave' (738). Olympio haughtily approves their new arrangement and Lysidamus further obliges him in sub-servient language tinged with (homo)eroticism: 'I'm at your service, my darling little Olympio, my father and patron' (738–9). In response to Olympio's approval, Lysidamus completes his surrender: 'I'm all yours' (741).

Changing the subject to Casina, Lysidamus asks his slave, 'How soon till you revive me?' (743). Olympio, starved and thirsty (725), construes this as referring to dinner preparations. Both then focus on food and of course the prospect of 'Cinnamon Girl', and reflecting their inverted roles, Lysidamus asks Olympio to order the train of cooks inside (745–6). Olympio now fully embraces his superior status by performing a pretentious, metacomic shtick. As Chytrio's crew parades into the house, Olympio imperiously shouts, 'I want dinner to be elegant and classy: I've got no stomach for barbarian slop' (747–7a). In Plautus, characters use *barbaricus* (and similar words) to mean 'Roman' as they humorously assume the attitude of Greeks, often in contexts bearing programmatic significance for Plautine comedy.[83] The lowly farm-manager is incongruously made to denigrate – no doubt ironically – Roman fare, both culinary and comic, from the perspective of a Greek cultural elite.

The scene's conclusion brings spectators back to immediate plot exigencies, (mis)understood as these are by both master and slave. Lysidamus informs Olympio of Casina's reported rage. Olympio at first is sceptical and (correctly) suspects that the women, whom he characterizes as a 'bad lot' (752), are up to something. He urges Lysidamus to go inside together with him, but the obviously frightened master wants his slave to reconnoitre for him (754–5). After further quarrelling and some physical shifting and shoving, Olympio delivers the scene's final command ('go in now') to his master, punctuated by Lysidamus's acquiescence: 'If you're ordering me, I'll go with you' (758). With their exit the stage is empty.

Some time has passed when Pardalisca exits from Lysidamus's house to deliver, in vivid present-tense narrative, a musically unaccompanied monologue. Pardalisca confirms that the women have established a gynocracy inside the house. She again performs a messenger's role (cf. **Scene 14**), though her report is truthful this time as spokesperson for Cleostrata's evolving plot. Pardalisca begins with a hyperbolic comparison:[84] the great athletic contests (*ludos*, 760) of Greece are no match for the 'playful games' (*ludi ludificabiles*, 761) at Lysidamus's and Olympio's expense inside. Pardalisca's use of *ludi* here points to a play-within-the-play, as is quickly confirmed when Pardalisca reveals that the women are secretly 'costuming' (769) Chalinus to be the bride Casina. The reference to competitive struggles between naked men, such as those at ancient Olympia and Nemea, also looks ahead to **Scenes 21–3**. The sex-starved Lysidamus is said to be demanding dinner (764–6). Pardalisca vividly reports the frustrated old man's speech as the cooks, now bit-players under the women's direction, purposely delay the feast and the old man's plot (772–5).

Pardalisca summarizes the plot's progress by neatly combining the metaphors of food, desire and satiation (see pp. 92–6):

> The ladies want
> To drive the old man out of the house without dinner,
> So they can be the ones to stuff their stomachs.
> They're *gourmandesses*, all right:
> They could gobble down a boatload of food!
>
>   775–9

With the women increasingly seizing control of both cuisine and the play, Pardalisca's colourful monologue concludes when she notices the door of the house opening.

Lysidamus appears, yelling back to Cleostrata inside and clearly frustrated by the caterers' delays, and he announces his (fictive) plan to accompany the newlyweds to his country estate while it is still light. Lysidamus will chaperone, ironically, 'so that no one abducts her' (784), that is, from himself and his violent intentions. In describing the couple as 'the new groom and new bride' (782), the Latin adjective *noua* with reference to Casina, whom the audience now knows is to be Chalinus, suggests the meaning, 'strange'. The Latin word for 'bride', *nupta* (a participle of *nubo*, 'to veil oneself (for a husband)'), refers to the flame-coloured veil worn by Roman brides; here, in connection with the bearded and burly Chalinus, it suggests 'the strangely veiled one'. The old man's confidence in his coded language is delusional: spectators can now easily guess that he won't be 'dining' apart from his wife (780–1) and that the 'country', as he describes Alcesimus's house, will prove a poor venue for his honeymoon. The eavesdropping Pardalisca confirms that Lysidamus has been evicted by the women from his own house without dinner (788–9). Lysidamus notices her as she finishes this aside, accuses her of spying on him and sends her into his house. Alone, Lysidamus asserts that he can say what he wants (794), erroneously assuming he has the audience's sympathy. Despite the build-up, he manages to utter only a cliché about love: 'Even if a lover's hungry, by god he feels no hunger' (795). The old man's monologue abruptly ends when he announces Olympio's entrance, coining a new word to describe the farm-manager as his 'co-husband' (*commaritus*, 797).

Here comes the elephant (Scenes 18–19)

As the music restarts, Olympio – still dressed in white and now sporting a bridegroom's floral garland and bearing a wedding torch (796) – in a delightful disruption of theatrical illusion solemnly implores the performance's piper[85] to play the wedding song: 'fill this entire street with the sweet wedding song' (799). He again metatheatrically refers to the 'strange bride' (798) and the street that is to resound with nuptial song is of course Roman comedy's stage. The ludicrous co-husbands together erupt into the ritual wedding cry. Lysidamus continues to fawn upon Olympio, addressing him as his 'saviour' (801). The earthy farm-manager again complains of hunger, while Lysidamus picks up where he left off at the previous scene's close by asserting that he is hungry only for love. Olympio mocks him and complains about his own rumbling intestines. After the pair enthusiastically repeat the wedding refrain to draw the women outside, Lysidamus makes a half-intelligible, obscene joke: 'I may burst myself from singing that before I get a chance to "burst" the disease I want to' (809–10). Olympio's apt comment, 'if you were a stallion, there'd be no chance of taming you', is met with another sexual advance by the old man: Lys. 'How do you mean?' Oly. 'You're way too intense.' Lys. 'But you've never taken a ride with me' (812). As Olympio curses this thought, the door of Lysidamus' house creaks and the old man foolishly reckons himself to be saved by the gods (814).

With Cleostrata following, Pardalisca leads Chalinus, the silent bride, to the groom.[86] Pardalisca's first words – 'Casinus[87] has already given off a scent from afar' (815–16) – neatly capture the situation. Blinded by their desire, the men have virtually fetishized 'Cinnamon Girl' into incorporeality, as an exotic scent qua sexual fantasy, and they are about to be struck by the physicality of her male replacement. Onstage, the opposing parties align themselves in a kind of battle formation, with Chalinus, the bride about to be transferred to the groom, in the middle of all. Chalinus is appropriately costumed in a long woollen, belted tunic, an orangish veil, orange-yellow slippers, and his hair may be elaborately braided.[88] The farce here can be augmented by retaining some marker of maleness, such as making Chalinus's beard visible beneath the translucent veil, and having him walk in an un-maiden-like style: 'part of the humor stems from Lysidamus being fooled by what is clearly a poor disguise.'[89]

Pardalisca's opening song, in offering advice to the bride, delightfully parodies Roman marriage ideals, down to details of sacral language,[90] as it also ominously foreshadows the scuffle among the men to come:

> Gently raise your feet above the threshold, my new bride;
> Safely commence this journey –
> *And stomp upon your husband always!*
> May all power be yours to crush and defeat him,
> Your voice, your command perched on high to beat him!
> His job's to stock your closets, yours to empty his pockets.
>
> 815–22

While the ritual admonishment to avoid stumbling over the threshold strikes a solemn note,[91] mention of the 'strange bride' (815–16) marks a swift transition to parody: in subversion of traditional nuptial language,[92] 'safe' (817) execution of this first step is said to lead to the bride's 'secure superiority' (818) over her husband, and the hope that she will be her husband's vanquisher (819–20).[93] Pardalisca offers a capping exhortation: 'May you never forget to deceive your husband day and night' (823–4). While Lysidamus remains rapt at the prospect of realizing his sexual fantasy and downplays any threat (825–8), Olympio grasps the menacing tenor of the song: 'a nasty woman's giving nasty advice to a nasty girl' (826). Pardalisca's formal utterance, 'Go on, Olympio, since you consent, take her as your wife from us' (829–30), completes the wedding ceremony.[94] Cleostrata delays the impatient men by urging gentle treatment of 'the inexperienced virgin' (832). The women finally exit into Lysidamus's house after a comically prolonged parting: Pard. 'Goodbye.' Oly. 'Go along now.' Lys. 'Do go.' Cleo. 'Goodbye now' (834).

Once he is convinced that his wife has gone, Lysidamus inaugurates the honeymoon farce by ironically declaring himself 'free' (837) and showering Chalinus with lover's endearments (839). Master and slave set to quarrelling over the bride, to whom Lysidamus claims first rights (839).[95] Olympio tries to force Lysidamus to hold his wedding torch, in order to free up his hands to grope Chalinus, but the old man has beat him to the punch (840). As the pair begin to engage in competitive fondling of Chalinus's 'tender little body', Olympio suddenly exclaims, 'my little wife, what's wrong?' (843–4) and reveals that the bride has stomped on his foot like an elephant (845–6). The bruiser Chalinus thus sets out on shattering the pair's illusion of the sixteen-year-old slave's alluring body being within their grasp.[96]

Following Lysidamus's order to Olympio to be quiet (846), the music suddenly stops, thus initiating the play's final musical arc (847–1018).[97] Lysidamus dismisses Olympio's complaint and compares Chalinus's breasts (favourably) with a soft cloud (847). His mirage restored, Olympio's attempt to caress Chalinus's nipple is rudely met with a powerful elbow to his chest (849). The parodic wedding scene thus concludes with a mere sampling of the violence that is to follow offstage. As Lysidamus chastises Olympio for his harsh handling of Chalinus, the farm-manager suffers another blow ('my goodness, she's a strong little one', 852), again from Chalinus's elbow (*cubito*, 853). Deluded by his belief in his own cleverness as a lover, Lysidamus nonchalantly puns, 'so she's pushy to go to bed' (*cubitum*, 853). The scene concludes with the old man's ill-conceived expression of affection to the bride: 'make your pretty way, my little pretty' (854). The three characters empty the stage by exiting into Alcesimus's house.

Director's cut (Scenes 20–2)

The empty stage promotes the idea of dramatic time having passed. When Myrrhina, Pardalisca and Cleostrata jubilantly emerge from Lysidamus's house, miming laughter as they take their places onstage, they announce that they have enjoyed a fine feast inside (855), thus bringing the play's running theme of food to a climax (see pp. 92–6). Myrrhina extends the metaphor of *ludi* used by Pardalisca in **Scene 16**: 'we've come out on the street here to watch the wedding games/ festival' (*ludos . . . nuptialis*, 856). As interested spectators, the women anxiously await the entrances of Olympio and Lysidamus, whose shame suffered within the house is about to be made public.[98] The designation of the farcical nuptials as *ludi* here highlights the role the women have assumed as creators of a play-within-the-play whose conclusion they will now watch as an internal audience (cf. 870–1). Myrrhina makes this metatheatrical dimension of their ruse explicit: 'no playwright has ever devised a cleverer plot than the one we've crafted here' (860–1). The audience has not seen Myrrhina since **Scene 3**, where she argued against Cleostrata's desire to seek retribution from her husband. We may readily assume that Cleostrata won her neighbour over to her cause offstage, perhaps by informing her of Alcesimus's making their house available for Lysidamus's sordid assignation: Cleostrata equates Alcesimus's culpability in the scheme with her own husband's (862–6). The characterization of the offstage follies of the men as 'nuptial games' anticipates the imminent appearance of the defeated Olympio and Lysidamus in **Scenes 21–2**. Pardalisca stresses the peculiar nature of this agonistic festival by referring to the newlyweds as 'he-bride and husband' (859).

Cleostrata makes it clear that she is the director of this show by placing Pardalisca close to the door of Alcesimus's house, so that she can immediately mock the men as they exit (866–8). The *matronae* stand just behind Pardalisca (872), to provide her support in speaking 'freely' (873), that is, in the manner of a free person to her master. No sooner do the three women set themselves in this strategic position than the door creaks. A panicked Olympio dashes out of Alcesimus's house without his cloak (934) and so wears only a tunic, the Roman equivalent of underwear. He does not notice the women until Pardalisca, at Cleostrata's insistence, moves closer and addresses him (892).

In his despairing song ('I don't know where to flee . . .', 875–6), Olympio openly reveals his disgrace, a state he claims is unprecedented for him (878). He is contrite and surprisingly employs traditional Roman moral vocabulary to condemn his behaviour (875–8). Despite his shame and fear, Olympio urges spectators to listen and learn from his negative example: 'it's worth your while to pay attention – the mess I made is ridiculous to hear and to recount' (879–80). Olympio's messenger speech (881–934) then commences, in which sections of text (as for much of the remainder of the play) are regrettably lost or damaged, some perhaps due to censorship. The 'strange bride' was led to a dark room in Alcesimus's house (881–2). There Olympio's efforts to beat his temporarily absent master to the punch by initiating foreplay with Chalinus fail (887–8a), as do his more forceful efforts behind a now bolted door ('I want to steal the task from the old man', 891). At this point Pardalisca, at Cleostrata's prompting, interrupts Olympio to sardonically ask him where his 'strange bride' (892) is. Olympio is shocked to learn he has been overheard, but Pardalisca presses him: 'What's happening inside? What's Casina up to? Is she being properly obedient?' (897–8).[99] The text of 900–8a is regrettably damaged, but after further goading from Pardalisca, Olympio resumes his account at a most challenging moment: while frisking his bride for a weapon, he grasped what felt like a sword's hilt, but which he now realizes was not because of its warmth (909–10). Far from finally accessing Casina's soft, voluptuous body and its (imagined) hidden delights, Olympio is forced to admit that he grabbed hold of something too large and vibrant to be an ordinary vegetable, such as a cucumber (912–14).[100] The true tenor of Pardalisca's tale of a sword-wielding Casina (**Scene 14**) is now obvious, and Olympio recounts what could easily have become his own rape, as Chalinus now is reported to have nearly enacted the phallic, castrating violence threatened in Pardalisca's narrative of a Bacchic Casina.

Pardalisca compels Olympio to continue still further. He obliges by reproducing his own direct speech imploring Casina to submit: 'please, my little wife, why are you treating your husband like this?' (917–20). Olympio's appeal to Chalinus's sense of wifely duty falls on deaf ears, as Chalinus blocks the farm-manager's attempts to have vaginal and then anal sex (921–6). Myrrhina sarcastically praises his narrative ('he's telling his story so elegantly', 927), which reaches its violent conclusion: for all his efforts, Olympio earns an injured lip (thanks to Chalinus's bristly beard) and suffers kicks to the chest followed by blows to his face. In this bedroom farce, not staged but vividly evoked through Olympio's words, sexual predator becomes helpless prey. Thoroughly defeated and demoralized, and now minus his cloak (932a), Olympio flees, leaving Chalinus to exact like justice from Lysidamus ('so that the old man'd drink from the same cup I did', 933–3a). As Pardalisca forces Olympio to agree that he and his master have been cleverly tricked, the door of Alcesimus's house creaks. The traumatized Olympio fears that it is Chalinus, but instead his discombobulated master emerges.

Cloak-less (945) and without his walking-stick (975), in comedy an icon of his privileged status as *paterfamilias*,[101] Lysidamus delivers his own monody of helplessness ('I don't know what to do in this mess of mine', 938), which stands in sharp contrast to his confident entrance song (**Scene 4**). Thoroughly unnerved, the *senex* does not notice the three women or Olympio onstage, and directly addresses the audience. Like Olympio before him, he notes his enormous disgrace (937), as well as the additional challenge of facing his wife (939–40, 944). Lysidamus's utter degradation might appear especially striking to those seated immediately before the stage, that is, senators. He initially determines to surrender to Cleostrata for corporal punishment, like a slave ('I'll offer her my back as punishment', 950), but then suddenly makes a desperate appeal to the spectators:

Anyone care to fill in for me here?
I'm fresh out of ideas, apart from
Playing the bad slave and hitting the road.
There's no hope for my shoulders in that house!

951–6

Even more degrading than surrendering to his wife for a beating, Lysidamus here contemplates assuming Roman society's lowest possible status by running away from his own house like a fugitive slave.[102] Lysidamus begins to flee, presumably toward the country wing, just as Chalinus calls him while exiting from Alcesimus's house: 'Now stop right there, lover!' (959–60). In a lame aside the terrified old man pretends not to hear, but Chalinus is hot on his trail.

Sticking it to him (Scene 23)

Chalinus, still wearing the bride's outfit that Olympio and Lysidamus were unable to remove and now also holding the old man's walking-stick and cloak, creates an amusing spectacle as he walks onstage for the play's denouement. All six of the main performers probably appear onstage here.[103] Chalinus opens by reproaching his master for his 'Massilian ways' (963; the men of the Greek colony of Marseille were stereotyped as pathics by Romans) and mockingly (perhaps in falsetto) urges Lysidamus to come back to bed and grope him (964–5).[104] The strikingly rare Latin verb Chalinus uses here (*subigitare*, 964) merits fleshing out: an iterative of *subigo* ('to drive, bring under'), it etymologically means 'to (repeatedly) force another to submit'.[105] It describes forceful action, always sexual in nature in Plautus,[106] where it specifically means 'to grope another man's woman', whether a purchased prostitute or a wife. Chalinus's ironic taunt points to key aspects of Lysidamus's illicit desire: the old man has utterly misconstrued the sexual claim he believes he has on Casina (now exposed as faux-female), especially as the real (that is, free) Casina properly belongs to someone else, in that she is to be his son's wife. Chalinus's verb thus glimpses not only the violence Casina might have suffered, but also the various legal and social violations at stake – rape of a free person, adultery of another man's betrothed/wife, disruption of a father–son relationship, and so on – in Lysidamus's pursuit of her.[107]

Chalinus thus boldly antagonizes Lysidamus, exploiting his character's ambiguous gender by mixing insincere blandishments with threats in appropriately exaggerated tones. The old man's walking-stick is weaponized when Chalinus threatens to beat his master with it (966).[108] His appropriation of the walking-stick thus visually emblematizes the complete social upheaval Lysidamus's obsession with Casina has created in his household. Cleostrata is the first of the women to speak when she steps forth from her eavesdropping position, followed closely by Pardalisca and Myrrhina, to acerbically greet Lysidamus as 'lover' (969; cf. Chalinus's address, 959–60).[109] Lysidamus now finds himself physically and proverbially trapped between the women ('dogs') and Chalinus ('wolves'), as he notes in an aside that wins him no sympathy (969–73): 'The spatial arrangement on stage aptly depicts Lysidamus's predicament as he stands stock still, centre stage; "caught in the act."'[110] The *senex* is utterly powerless before his wife, his slave and their allies. Myrrhina joins in the abuse – 'How are you, bigamist?' – as Cleostrata notes his dishevelled and nearly naked appearance (974–5). Pardalisca piles on the agony by asserting that Lysidamus must have lost his cloak and walking-stick during his adulterous sex romp with Chalinus (976). Chalinus chimes in, 'Aren't we going back to bed? I'm Casina' (977), no doubt punctuated with mock-seductive gestures. Cleostrata presses Lysidamus to account for the lost cloak, and the old man foolishly attempts to blame Bacchants (see pp. 32–4).

The text is then badly damaged, but Lysidamus apparently admits to his misbehaviour and utter humiliation (982–90). Even Olympio joins the public shaming of the *senex* by chastising Lysidamus for begging him to marry Casina (992–5).[111] Lysidamus makes one last feeble attempt to deny his bad behaviour, asking the women: 'Did I really do the things you say?' (996). Cleostrata glares at him incredulously: 'You even ask?' (997). With his wife and all the actors onstage menacingly aligned against him, Lysidamus is forced to offer a conditional apology: 'If I really did those things, then, damn it, I did wrong' (997). Cleostrata promises to remind Lysidamus of his misdeeds should his memory fail him in the future and directs him toward the house (998). Regaining some confidence at his wife's hint of forgiveness, Lysidamus steps closer to her and makes a kind of contractual pledge:[112]

> But, my wife, forgive your husband now. Myrrhina, ask Cleostrata
>   for me;
> If henceforth I ever lust after Casina or just start to lust for her,
> If henceforth I ever (to say nothing of lusting after her) do any such
>   deed,
> You, my wife, have every right to hang me up and whip me.
>   1000–3

Cleostrata's right to reassume her current mastery over Lysidamus, should he stray again, is thus conditionally extended into the post-play world, though it is difficult for spectators to believe that he is sincere and not merely acting out of expediency in the moment.[113] But for now, and for purposes of comic closure, Cleostrata is merciful: in yet another surprising twist in the treatment of comic types, Lysidamus now assumes the posture of a clever slave and is granted forgiveness at play's end.[114] Likewise, the play's actual triumphant trickster, Cleostrata, must seem to transition back to her traditional and quiet role as *materfamilas*.

As the audience awaits Cleostrata's response to Lysidamus's petition, the traditionalist Myrrhina urges her friend to forgive him. Cleostrata agrees to do so, but only for a metatheatrical reason:[115]

> I'll do as you say.
> But the only reason I'm letting you off the hook this easy
> Is that this play's long enough and I don't want to make it longer.
>
> 1004–6

Cleostrata then assures Lysidamus that she is no longer angry, and he declares her the most charming of wives (1008). Her return of Lysidamus's cloak and walking-stick metonymically marks a swift return to the domestic status quo. Still, the conditional nature of Lysidamus's 'self-control contract' and the directorial decision Cleostrata makes to forgive him to end the play leave some doubt as to whether Lysidamus truly is again in charge of his household. Nor does this harmonious yet arbitrary ending inspire much confidence that the old man, imaginatively projected into a post-dramatic world, will reform and always practise self-control. While traditional Roman family values at least appear to be restored, Chalinus is given the play's final, comic words:

> Damn it, I have been woefully wronged:
> I married two men, but neither one did his duty for his
> new/strange bride!
>
> 1010–11

There is no indication in Plautus's text that the characters then exit inside, and so they all apparently remain onstage for the play's epilogue (1012–18).

Loose ends and looser morals (epilogue)

There is no consensus as to who speaks the brief epilogue of *Casina*:

> Spectators, we're here to tell you what will happen inside.
> This Casina will be found out to be the next-door neighbours' daughter
> And she'll marry our young master, Euthynicus.
> Now the proper thing for you all to do is to give us the props you
>   rightfully owe us:
> Whoever does will hire the whore of his choice without his wife's
>   knowledge.
> But whoever doesn't clap loudly with everything he's got
> Will end up with a he-goat soaked in sewage instead of that whore.
>
> 1012–18

There is some, but by no means decisive, manuscript evidence for the delivery of Plautine epilogues by the entire comic troupe. In some instances, it seems clear that the character who speaks last in the play's final scene also delivers this extra-dramatic commentary, which is always combined with a call for applause.[116] We unfortunately do not know if the speakers of epilogues in Roman comedy removed their masks to most clearly mark closure,[117] which would 'bookend' the use of an unmasked actor to deliver the prologue. Here the reference to Euthynicus as 'our young master' (1014) indicates that the speaker is a household slave, most probably Chalinus, who spoke last in the play proper, though some editors give the epilogue to Pardalisca, who last spoke at 976. With either attribution, the interests of the play's fictive slave *familia* effectively merge with those of the acting troupe, also primarily composed of slaves, when the speaker urges spectators to

complete the theatrical transaction between actors and spectators by
applauding.

Dramatic epilogues provide playwrights with the opportunity to
tie up dramatic and ideological loose ends, and to get in the last word
about how they want audiences to receive their plays.[118] The final lines
of *Casina* are in fact loaded with these typical functions of epilogues.
First and foremost, the epilogue provides cover for Plautus's suppression of a standard New Comedy recognition scene, in which
Casina's free identity as the exposed infant of Alcesimus and Myrrhina
was revealed, and her engagement to Euthynicus arranged, with their
marriage perhaps even represented onstage at the end of Diphilus's
play.[119] The specific revelation that the fictional Casina will legitimately
marry (1014) recalls the prologue speaker's promise that a very real
actor who might have played this Casina will be available for faux-
marriage, that is prostitution, after the performance (84–7; see
pp. 39–40). The epilogue's close again brings prostitution to the
forefront (1016–18). There of course is no way to gauge audience
reactions to all of this, and these most probably were quite diverse.
Casina at any rate, in its round defeat of Lysidamus, has delivered its
promise not to represent illicit sexual activity (82).

The final joke, which suggests that married men who applaud
enthusiastically will be rewarded with 'the whore of their desire'[120]
without their wives' knowledge, is not as inconsistent with the play's
resounding condemnation of Lysidamus's lechery as it might at first
seem to modern readers. Lysidamus's worst moral straying lies in his
infatuation with a (now revealed to be) free person not available for
the kind of sexual exploitation he desires. In the elite Roman moral
tradition, sexual liaisons with low- or no-status prostitutes, provided
these remained free of emotional attachment and did not incur
financial liability, seem not to have been viewed as destabilizing
domestic life and might even be quietly overlooked by *matronae* (see
pp. 81–3). This, to us at least, cynical view of Roman marriage seems

to prevail in the epilogue. Nonetheless, the fantastical threat against married men in the audience who do not applaud loudly – that they will find themselves in bed with a stinking goat instead of an alluring prostitute (1018) – conjures up an image of the play's 'nuptial games', in which the malodorous and grotesquely lascivious Lysidamus ended up in bed with his hirsute 'strange bride'.[121] We can only wonder what husbands and wives, as well as other spectators, discussed once *Casina* ended.

Main Themes

Much of *Casina*'s appeal, both in Plautus's day and in ours, arises from its compelling articulation of such fundamentally human themes as desire, sex, gender and power. While the play and its characters are driven by the monstrous appetites of the narcissistic Lysidamus, *Casina* still has much to say about how these central aspects of individual and social experience shape our prospects for happiness. On the stage of patriarchal Rome, Plautus provocatively makes a woman emerge as a comic hero out of all the domestic havoc her husband wreaks.

Sexuality and sexual violence

Discussion of sexuality in *Casina* must begin with a broad outline of Roman sexual mores, especially as these differ from modern Western norms.[1] Roman male sexuality is characterized by its blatant phallocentricism and is governed by rules of dominance and submission. Above all else, protocols of male sexuality and masculinity required a Roman citizen to be the insertive party in sexual acts and never to be penetrated himself.[2] Relationships of power, based mainly on status and gender, thus were paramount in sex and defined sexual acts. An adult male citizen might have access to sexual relationships with (in addition to his wife) both his male and female slaves, prostitutes, his freedmen and freedwomen and foreigners, so long as his body remained inviolable, that is, sexually unpenetrated. A citizen who allowed himself to be sexually penetrated risked enormous public disgrace. The Roman citizen/slave owner thus completely controlled the bodies of his subordinates, who as property had no will or say in such matters. The law protected only free-born boys and free females of all ages (including of course other citizens' wives) from sexual assault. These were punishable acts of *stuprum* ('illicit sex'), which the prologue speaker promises Casina will not suffer in the play (82–3). Olympio in recounting his nuptials with Chalinus to the women seems to breach verisimilitude when he says, 'I ask her for a kiss as foreplay to *stuprum*' (887), as from his point of view sex with his bride is not illicit.[3] Some anxiety also seems to have surrounded a citizen's preference to engage in (insertive) sex with an older male, whose body was no longer smooth like a youth's and who had the ability to grow a full beard.[4]

Perhaps unsurprisingly, for Roman women there was a double standard regarding adultery, as wives were not permitted the sexual freedoms their husbands enjoyed. Wives ideally were expected to be chaste, virtuous and submissive to their husbands' will, and any extramarital sexual activity (including with slaves) exposed was likely to result in divorce, possible forfeiture of dowry and other penalties.[5] In Plautus's *Mercator* (817–29) an elderly female slave expounds upon the inequities of the Roman double standard:[6]

> If only husbands had to obey the same law as wives!
> A wife who's a good woman is content with a single husband;
> Why should a husband be any less content with a single wife?
>
> 823–5

That such circumspection found its way into a Plautine comedy suggests that some Roman women were well aware of the double standard and might be perturbed by their husbands' extramarital behaviour, even if they had no legal recourse against it. When Myrrhina urges her friend to tolerate Lysidamus's sexual whims as long as he provides for her (206–7), Cleostrata vehemently objects: 'Are you out of your mind? Why do you speak against your own interests?' (208–9). This can be taken as an indication that Cleostrata values her husband's marital fidelity and has strong feelings about his extramarital aspirations. To moderns conditioned to the idea of marriage as a romantic choice, the existence of such emotions in arranged marriages may seem counter-intuitive, especially when a husband has such easy access to multiple sex partners and seemingly unlimited power to pursue these sexual relationships with impunity, as Roman men did. There is in fact evidence (literary, documentary and inscriptional, especially on tombstones) that some Roman spouses sought emotional companionship, mutual respect and intimacy, including sexually, from their marriages.[7]

The sexual excesses and eccentricities of Lysidamus stand out prominently in *Casina*. In contrast, we learn virtually nothing about the desires of those enmeshed in all the sexual chaos the old man generates. Casina of course does not appear in the play and remains voiceless, save for the constructions of her that other characters create (see pp. 89–91). Euthynicus likewise never appears, though the prologue speaker informs us that his desire for Casina matches his father's (48–9). The further description of the young man's hope to add 'what he loves to his homestead' (lit. 'to his horse/cattle stall') hardly inspires ideas of romantic infatuation – Euthynicus, however, unlike his father, has the comically acceptable excuse of being young, male and stereotypically impulsive.[8] Cleostrata, as is expected of a respectable *matrona*, never explicitly expresses her personal feelings about her marital relationship with Lysidamus; we only see her soberly resisting Lysidamus's insincere coaxing efforts to mollify her in their first encounter (229–33). Olympio shows obvious erotic interest in Casina throughout the play, though he never manifests his master's utter lack of self-control and degree of obsession with her.

Lysidamus is an altogether different animal: Cleostrata dubs her husband a 'grey-haired gnat' (239) and Lysidamus and his neighbour

'castrated old rams' (535); Chalinus's choice of a proverb associates the
old man and Olympio with wild boars (476); Alcesimus, angry for
implicating Myrrhina in Lysidamus's plot, calls his friend 'a worthless,
toothless goat' (550); as his master champs at the bit just before
the wedding, Olympio comments, 'if you were a stallion, there'd be
no taming you' (811).[9] Through such imagery alone there emerges a
picture of an annoyingly aggressive and lecherous, if decrepit and
impotent beast of a human being. Lysidamus lacks all self-control in
a manner, to Roman male elite thinking, unbefitting of his age and
status. The *senex*'s failure to control his desires and emotions (for
example, 'poor me, I'm utterly tortured by love', 276) suggests the softness
and frailty of youth, not the firm resolution mature Roman men are
expected to project at all times. The absence of sexual control was
readily assumed to be accompanied by a host of other weaknesses.[10]
Cleostrata supposes such a moral slippery slope when, after detecting
the perfumed hair-oil with which the old man hopes to attract Casina
(240), she accuses Lysidamus of drinking and frequenting brothels,
and sarcastically exhorts him, 'By all means go ahead and do what you
want: drink, eat, squander your money!' (248).

Lysidamus's extreme sexuality is most clearly seen in his amorous
interaction with Olympio once they win the lottery (451–71).
According to Roman mores, there is nothing aberrant about a master's
sexual advances toward a male slave per se, but as the eavesdropping
Chalinus comments after revealing Lysidamus's past assault against
himself, 'this old man really loves to chase after the ones with beards'
(466). Chalinus highlights this irregular aspect of Lysidamus's lust, as
the old man does himself by bracketing the exchange with the rare
verb *deosculor* ('to kiss deeply') in reference to both the adult, bearded
Olympio (453) and the delicate, young Casina (467), thus treating the
two as interchangeable objects of his lechery.[11] And an uncomfortable,
if ambiguous, spectre of criminality surrounds the old man's pursuit
of Casina. Even if a master's desire to exploit a young female slave

raised few or no eyebrows, spectators know from the start that Casina is a freeborn Athenian (81–2), kept chaste and raised like a daughter by Lysidamus's wife (46), who also wants to protect and preserve Casina for her son. Lurking beneath the old man's lust and the Plautine sex farce, then, is the incestuous and potentially tragic pursuit of a quasi-daughter or daughter-in-law.[12] The lengths to which Lysidamus goes to conceal his designs on Casina,[13] however ineptly executed, certainly indicate that he knows his behaviour is inappropriate and must be concealed from his wife.

Perhaps the most excessive and disturbing aspect of Lysidamus's excessive sexuality and the complications it creates for others is its persistent association with violence. Because of Lysidamus's obsessive character, there is no other extant Roman comedy in which the prospect of sexual violence is so pervasive and looming as it is in *Casina*. As he and Olympio eagerly await the wedding, Lysidamus himself comes to describe his overwhelming desire for Casina as a kind of sickness, when he struggles to turn a joke about his level of sexual excitement: 'I may burst myself from singing that before I get a chance to "burst" the disease I want to' (809–10).[14] Lysidamus had used the same crude sexual euphemism[15] with reference to Cleostrata after Olympio informed him that she was seething with anger: 'I'd like to see her split right down the middle' (326–7). When the slaves are egged on to an exchange of blows during the lottery, we witness a thinly veiled scene of domestic battery between spouses (see p. 51). Chalinus graphically describes Lysidamus's physical affection for Olympio as his master's wish 'to burrow into the bailiff's bladder' (455). Lysidamus threatens to pulverize Pardalisca's skull with his walking-stick after she sexually teases him (644–5). The tables are abruptly turned on the old man and Olympio after the wedding, when the bride-in-drag subjects them to humiliating violence that includes the threat of sexual penetration by Chalinus's erect penis-sword (909–14). Decorum in a society in which masters' bodies must remain inviolable prevents the representation, either onstage or in (offstage) reported narrative, of Lysidamus suffering a beating or sexual violation, but Olympio's description of his experience with Chalinus is suggestive enough. His attempts to penetrate the bride Chalinus vaginally and anally are met with violent kicks and painful pricks from Chalinus's beard (929–31a). Olympio then makes a point of saying that he abruptly fled to cause his master to suffer the same treatment from the bride (932a–3a). We are then treated to the finale (**Scene 23**) in which Chalinus playfully threatens Lysidamus with his phallic walking-stick-turned-club, which, the old man frantically fears, will 'depilate his loins' (967), that is, completely emasculate him.[16]

Lysidamus necessarily escapes any actual violence, sexual or otherwise, in the play's denouement. But his humiliation and the highly visible threats of a physical assault against him unquestionably remind spectators of 'the degradation and violence that Casina might have experienced ... had not Cleostrata changed the course of the play'.[17] Modern scholars understandably are overwhelmed by the brutality of Roman slavery and its hard-line ideology supporting the idea of 'natural slaves', in other words, those, as Aristotle claimed, who were by birth inferior and something other than fully human, devoid of will and reason, and for practical purposes usually invisible. But while ancient Roman society for centuries lived comfortably with the naturalization of slavery (Varro infamously designated a slave 'a tool with a voice'), many free persons at times must have found themselves forced to acknowledge some aspects of a slave's humanity. By similar oversimplification, scholars also tend to reduce Plautus's audience to a monolithic block, usually assumed to support the dominant elite's ideology, even though we know the spectatorship of Plautine plays included a diverse array of Roman society, including slaves.[18] It thus seems overly dogmatic to assume that no one in Plautus's audience had any second thoughts about the sexual violence Lysidamus might have inflicted on Casina. The fact that she wasn't really a slave and in the end fortuitously escapes sexual violence only further problematizes the matter, as Romans knew from experience that free persons were often enslaved by chance (as prisoners of war, victims of kidnapping, and so on). Furthermore, in his closing assurances that Casina would be discovered to be freeborn and escape sexual assault 'in this comedy' (83), the prologue speaker had also invited spectators to consider the post-play sexual exploitation, in the form of prostitution, of the low-status actor who might have played Casina, had she been a character in the play (84–6). The imaginative world of the play and its characters, even as this is largely de-romanticized by Plautus, and that of the actors who create it uncomfortably collide in this seemingly gratuitous reference to the actors' vulnerable existence.[19] The world outside the theatre unfortunately is full of men like Lysidamus.

The performance of gender

Issues of gender permeate *Casina*, which generally recalls the 'women on top' plays of Aristophanes (*Lysistrata*, *Women at the Thesmophoria*, *Assemblywomen*) in that the female characters step out of their traditionally restricted roles in an effort to correct the misbehaviour of men. Traditional gender stereotypes are destabilized in the course of *Casina*, as the *paterfamilias* Lysidamus falls far short of the omnipotent Jupiter figure (230a, 331) he imagines himself to be, and undergoes a complete degradation of status in the play owing to his wife's machinations. Cleostrata, while never claiming the queen of the gods' status for herself (cf. 230, 408), in *Casina* becomes a triumphant Juno to Lysidamus's impotent Jove. The absent figure of Casina also evokes a fascinating jumble of gender-related issues as she is variously constructed by the play's characters.

The prologue speaker introduces the notion of a 'battle of the sexes' (see pp. 37–8), though he gives spectators little idea as to what

particular form this will take. Those conversant with Roman comedy
might expect the familiar scenario of a pleasure-seeking husband
whose desires are at every turn opposed by his dowered, hyper-
vigilant and shrewishly unsympathetic wife, as in, for example,
Plautus's *Menaechmi*.[20] Lysidamus unsuccessfully encourages the
audience to see his wife (and *Casina*) in this straightforwardly
misogynistic way. After declaring love to be the spice of life in his
flamboyant entrance song, Lysidamus finally notices that Cleostrata is
present and comments in an aside: 'My wife tortures me with her very
breath – look at her standing there so sour. Time to sweet talk the
nasty thing' (227–8). He dismisses Cleostrata's subsequent complaints
about his extravagant (mis)behaviour by ordering her to get control
of herself (!), stop 'making [his] ears ring' and to 'save some of her
complaints for tomorrow' (249–51). Lysidamus bitterly complains
that while he is being tortured by love, 'she makes it her business to
oppose [him]' (276–7). With his ally-in-lust Olympio, Lysidamus
jokes that his wife is 'a 24/7 hunting-bitch' (319–20) and a garrulous
'tongue-fish' (497–8). Lysidamus's final attempt (in an aside) to cast
his wife as a proverbial bitch is hopelessly inept, as he now stands
nearly naked and entirely humiliated onstage (971–3).

Early in the play, Myrrhina, fittingly provided with a distaff for
wool-working,[21] is made to represent the traditional wife – verbally
guarded, subservient to her husband and tolerant of his misdeeds
(see pp. 43–4) – that Lysidamus clearly wishes Cleostrata were. This
traditional stereotype, however, appears only to be invoked so that it
can be wholly shattered by Cleostrata and even Myrrhina in that she
ultimately joins the theatrical conspiracy against the philandering
Lysidamus.[22] Cleostrata gives a strong indication that she may upset
and challenge gender expectations in her first action onstage. The
opening words of her song (directed back at slaves inside the house),
'Lock the pantry and give me the keys', part of her plan to 'starve' her
husband both literally and figuratively (see p. 42), would certainly

catch spectators' attention as brash in that her specific demands immediately locate her on culturally dangerous ground.[23]

Cleostrata gradually assumes complete control of both her husband and the play when she authors the plan to dress Chalinus as the bride Casina. The women's play-within-the-play is so resoundingly successful that Lysidamus is made to gradually voluntarily surrender all his masculine privilege and reputed inviolability in **Scenes 22-3**. There he declares his willingness to offer his back to his wife for servile punishment (949-50), considers flight like a runaway slave (952-60), and wagers his own body in contracting to never again pursue Casina (1001-3). As perhaps an even further degradation, he feels compelled to declare Cleostrata 'the most charming wife' (1008), thus effectively repudiating all his earlier misogynistic insults against her as well as his previous claims to being a charming lover himself (see p. 45). Of course, well before his final defeat Lysidamus himself contributes to the abasement of his (Roman) masculinity.[24] For example, he impulsively threatens suicide by his sword after he unnecessarily fears that Cleostrata has talked Olympio out of pursuing the marriage with Casina (304-8). His fixation on realizing the plan for a sexual ambush of Casina in Alcesimus's house leads him to chastise his wife for not employing more coaxing speech to his neighbour – like a prostitute, as Cleostrata points out – in persuading Alcesimus to send his wife to their house (584-6).[25] We also witness Lysidamus pandering to Pardalisca for assistance in dealing with the allegedly raging Casina (704-12) and chalking up his failure to advocate successfully in his relative's legal dispute to his own infatuation with Casina (563-73).

One of Plautus's most brilliant moves in *Casina* is to leave the title-character out of the play – and to give her the name 'Cinnamon-Girl'.[26] *Casina* as a result engages in some of Plautus's most delightful metatheatrical play, while also exposing some of the instabilities in Roman configurations of gender. 'Casina', as the mental object of the hyperactive male gaze, is elaborately constructed despite her absence.[27]

For the men who desire her, Casina will remain only an alluring, but elusive aroma. Largely a projection of testosterone-fogged memory, Casina becomes a delicate, soft and diminutive creation: 'pretty and tender little Casina' (108), as Olympio initially describes her. The farm-manager is also the first character to bestow a voice upon Casina, when he optimistically imagines her speaking directly to him in intimate terms of endearment (134–8; see pp. 40–1). In her messenger's speech, Pardalisca assigns a dramatically different voice and deviant personality to Casina. In fabricating her tale of a raving-mad, sword-wielding Casina who refuses to comply with the marriage plan, Pardalisca first (indirectly) quotes Casina as saying she'll kill whoever sleeps with her tonight (668–71). Exploiting Lysidamus's obvious fear for himself (revealed by his Freudian slip about Casina's murderous plans being directed at him, 672–5), Pardalisca gives the Casina of her narrative a second sword and now offers a more precise version of the slave's threatening words: 'she says she'll kill you with one of the swords and the farm-manager with the other today' (692–3). Spectators, now deeply implicated in Casina's creation, have sharply conflicting notions of her to imagine.[28]

These two Casinas form the backdrop of Chalinus's climactic impersonation of Casina, that is, as a male actor playing a male character playing a female slave, in the wedding scene and its aftermath. Once the parodic ceremony is performed and Chalinus, appropriately costumed in bridal apparel, is delivered to Olympio and his master, the competing constructions of the slave collide most violently. Chalinus's unsurprising acting choice is to play Casina as a hyper-masculinized, fierce agent of revenge, a role ridiculously made evident in performance by the obvious 'manly' flaws in his bridal attire.[29] The sexually excited Lysidamus and Olympio nonetheless stay committed to their idea of Casina, which they continue to forge as they escort the newlywed Chalinus to bed. Just as Olympio begins to admiringly approve his 'little wife's tender little body' (843–4), Chalinus stamps on his foot with the force of an elephant. The distracted Lysidamus dismisses Olympio's cry of pain and declares Chalinus's chest to be softer than a cloud (847). Joining in with praise of the bride's 'pretty little nipple', Olympio is stopped in his tracks by a powerful elbow to his own chest (848–9). Lysidamus again assuages Olympio, and as the trio exit toward what will prove to be a bedroom of horrors at Alcesimus's house, the scene ends with the old man's optimistic address to Chalinus as his 'pretty little pretty' (854). Olympio is forced by the women to provide essential details of the travesties of gender that take place inside (**Scene 21**). Though he admits to grabbing hold of a large and warm object he tentatively identifies as a sword's hilt during his scuffle with Chalinus (909–14), Olympio does not yet fully grasp the women's plot, as he is made to miss or ignore other clues such as the bride's beard. He reports (in direct speech) his efforts to coax his 'little wife' into sexual submission, at which Chalinus-Casina remains ominously silent (917–21). The latter then defends what Olympio believes to be his wife's vagina, which in turn leads the farm-manager to launch an unsuccessful and forcibly repulsed assault on Chalinus's anus (922–31a). Humiliated, dazed and confused by the experience, Olympio now seems not to realize that he barely escaped rape by the far from delicate, physically superior and fully erect Chalinus. It is left to Lysidamus, as he is physically menaced onstage by the club-wielding Chalinus (**Scene 23**), to more explicitly acknowledge the virtual rape and castration both master and slave suffer (see pp. 73–7). Chalinus, beckoning his master (perhaps in falsetto) to come back to bed, succinctly captures the play-within-the-play's main transformation of gender: 'I'm Casina' (977). The harried old man is thus invited to an inverse honeymoon, where the sex he had so intensely planned for Casina is to be inflicted upon him by her male surrogate.

It is for various reasons inadvisable to claim with confidence that Plautus or the play target(s) elite Roman norms of masculinity or (anachronistically) advances a feminist agenda about these here. We can, however, reasonably speak of a pervasively constructivist outlook in Plautine comedy. Theatre, because it traffics in the creation of roles and worlds, is to some extent always focused on the artifice of human behaviour and society in general and so by its very nature holds socially subversive potential. But as the elaborate creation of Casina/Casinus demonstrates, this constructivist tendency seems especially pronounced in Plautus, where, for example, by a familiar trope clever slaves who pull off a successful caper loudly stake their claim to the honours and status of Roman aristocratic generals at the opposite extreme of the social hierarchy.[30] Audiences no doubt were amused by such inversions because of the incongruities involved, and had become conditioned to laugh at them, but they may also suggest (to some at least) that the world outside the theatre is highly performative. Is a general destined to celebrate a Roman triumph owing to his birthright, privilege, aristocratic lineage and essential character, or could it also be about his look, swagger, attitude, costume, saying certain words and following a social script, as well as inherited status and power? The same sorts of questions in regard to gender might occur to some of *Casina's* spectators after watching Chalinus so blatantly cross established lines in order to create his Casina. Just how stable were the rigid categories of gender so vigorously prescribed and upheld by the male elite? Plautine comedy seems to pose such questions, and it does not seem absurd to imagine some theatregoers being induced to consider these themselves.

Food, desire, scents and sense

Casina offers a cornucopia of culinary themes and metaphors that are often intricately combined with motifs of sexuality and gender. Casina's very name associates her with a highly aromatic and alluring condiment,[31] and Cleostrata early on states her intent to punish her husband's sexual fixation on Casina 'with hunger and thirst' (155–6). *Casina*'s audience is bombarded with foods and scents, as spectators are repeatedly challenged to activate their gastronomic and olfactory memories as they process the action. While associations of food and its aromas with appetite/desire are widespread across cultures and literatures, *Casina* often articulates these in surprising ways. Examination of *Casina*'s particular tastes and smells also provides further insights into the play's characters, their motivations and their overall (a)sociability.

Cleostrata's gradual control of Lysidamus and his animal appetites is mirrored by her ability to keep him from eating. Sex and food, like 'Cinnamon Girl' herself, are only immaterial scents for the *senex amator*, whose appetites for both were supposed to have cooled at his age.[32] As Cleostrata creatively and aptly puts it, the old man is himself 'death-chow' (159).[33] But because Lysidamus remains so preternaturally ravenous, Cleostrata, perhaps naively assuming that the denial of one of his desires will suppress them all, must take the unusual measures of locking the pantry and refusing to prepare the lunch he has demanded (144–50). We soon see how smitten Lysidamus is, both in terms of food and sex, when he first enters: love, he avows, is the ultimate spice that improves any dish.[34] A dash of love can transform bile into honey or even a grumpy old man into someone 'charming and chill' (*lepidum et lenem*, 223) – that is, a sprinkle of love accompanied by a dousing of cologne (236–41), according to the deluded old man. For Olympio and Lysidamus, the acquisition of Casina's body is equated with a lavishly catered feast (490–501), both of which they assume will sate their desires. But as the women's plan to starve the pair progresses, it becomes clear that the appetites of master and slave are of different orders. Whereas Olympio continuously complains about his literal hunger (725, 801–4), his master is so enslaved by his lust for Casina that he is willing to forgo food: 'By golly, even if a man in love is hungry, he doesn't feel his hunger' (797).[35] The old man tacitly accepts the women's plan to 'toss him out of his house without dinner' (789) by agreeing to delay his dinner to the next day (780–7) because he is blissfully unaware of the plot they have concocted against him.[36] Neither Lysidamus nor Olympio is ever fed, and we learn that the women co-opted the nuptial feast planned for Alcesimus's house for themselves. Pardalisca describes Cleostrata and Myrrhina as 'gourmandesses' who 'alone will stuff their bellies' (777–8); it is in such a sated condition that the women eventually emerge onstage to enjoy the fruits of their theatrical labours (855).[37]

The notion that food can become an instrument of torture runs throughout *Casina*. In the play's very first scene, Olympio fantasizes about lording over Chalinus on the farm once he has married Casina. The farm-manager's plan is to assign tortuous tasks to Chalinus all day while also depriving him of food:

> And when you'd like a bite to eat,
> You can feast yourself on some fodder
> Or eat dirt like a worm. I'll see that you're hungrier
> Than Hunger itself out there in the sticks.
>
>   126–9

The 'exhausted and famished' (130) Chalinus's excruciating days will be capped by nights in which he is sadistically forced to watch the newlyweds' lovemaking while bound to their bedroom window (132–40).[38] Olympio gruesomely tells Cleostrata that he'd rather be baked in an oven like biscotti than relinquish his claim to Casina (309–11). Chalinus punningly imagines the sole-fish Lysidamus requests for the nuptial feast transforming into the soles of clogs that could smash the old man's face (495–7). This weaponization of food culminates in the women's successful 'food-strike' against Lysidamus and Olympio: after Olympio divulges his grabbing hold of what seemed like his bride's warm 'sword-hilt', Pardalisca demands to know if the object was a radish or a cucumber (911). In the women's exquisite plot, even vegetables threaten to morph into tools of phallic punishment.

Food and aromas can be highly sexual and gendered in *Casina*. Pardalisca by her very name, 'Little Panther', is associated with a dangerous and alluring scent, as the panther's sweet breath was believed to attract its prey; she obviously acts as a seductive predator toward Lysidamus during her fictional messenger's speech.[39] Imagining a utopian banquet of food and sex, Lysidamus requests market items that mirror his image of Casina: 'I want fine delicacies because she's so delicate herself' (491–2). The bride Chalinus will of course represent a very different kind of fare. Both Olympio (135) and Lysidamus (837) figure Casina as their 'little honey', while the old man's extraordinary lust is highlighted by his proclamation that hugging Olympio is like licking honey (458). Just before the nuptial violence ensues, Lysidamus ironically claims the 'first fruits' (839) from Casina. The males in the play by contrast tend to be associated with unpleasant odours. Lysidamus's having drenched himself with cologne apparently does not disguise the smell of alcohol in his first encounter with Cleostrata (246), who simultaneously perceives his moral stench: 'You worthless man, promenading through town soaked in cologne' (239). Olympio's strong revulsion at the old man's breath (727) suggests that it is more redolent of bile than honey.[40] Pardalisca's comment, 'Casinus has already given off a scent from afar' (815–16), mocks the men's subjective ideation of 'Cinnamon Girl' (see pp. 68, 89–91), but may also encourage spectators to think of Chalinus – as he now appears onstage as a burly bride in a poor disguise – emitting a strongly unhygienic 'masculine' odour.[41] The stinking he-goat with which the epilogue of *Casina* closes (1118) leaves the audience with a final foul smell to imagine in connection with sex.

Finally, cooking serves as a metaphor for plotting in *Casina*. At a major turning point in the play, Chalinus overhears Lysidamus's plans for the nuptial feast at Alcesimus's house. Elated by this revelation, Chalinus riffs on Lysidamus's order for foodstuffs:

> I'll going inside to add a different spice of my own
> To what that cook's got simmering.
> The meal he thinks is ready for him won't be served,
> And as for what's to be served up for him – there's no way he's ready
> for that!

511–14

Though it is unclear what spice Chalinus intends to add to the comic stew, spectators can be confident that something now is afoot to frustrate Lysidamus's desires. They may not suspect that Cleostrata as well as Chalinus is involved in the plotting, as generic expectations point to the slave, not the *matrona*, cooking up some kind of trick (cf. pp. 97–9). Regardless, the connection between cooking and plotting is familiar enough in Plautus, where the figure of the cook may serve as an authorial stand-in.[42] A key element in the women's plot is soon revealed to be their seizing control of the cooks and caterers, who are made to intentionally delay their tasks and ultimately to divert the feast to the women (772–8). In this way, the women's roles as cooks and directors of the play-within-the-play are delightfully mixed.

Cleostrata the comic heroine

Cleostrata emerges as the play's decisive winner. On the basis of significant names alone, her ultimate triumph perhaps is not surprising: the 'glory' of a female 'army' (see p. 37) aided by a cross-dressing military-man[43] prevails, and her conquest is heralded by the long-delayed revelation of the beneficiary of her efforts' name, Euthynicus, or 'Direct-Victory' (1014). The assertive and independent Cleostrata, a kind of Lysistrata in the domestic sphere, has successfully led a solidarity movement to defeat her foolish, phallocentric and philandering husband. Moreover, in contrast to Plautus's carping, domineering and humourless dowered wives, Cleostrata is an intelligent, creative and judiciously bold woman who unambiguously occupies the moral high ground in *Casina*. She unquestionably is *Casina*'s most sympathetic and controlling character and so its comic heroine, as is brilliantly made clear when at the play's end she forgives Lysidamus because the play is already long enough (1005-6). Cleostrata's arbitrary and metatheatrical choice here also closes down the possibility of any serious, enduring resolution to her fraught domestic situation.[44] What exactly then has Cleostrata's elaborate ruse and her punishment of Lysidamus accomplished?

As we have seen throughout, *Casina*, a most sophisticated late play of a sophisticated comic playwright, features surprising manipulations of New Comedy's stock characters and situations.[45] Most significantly, the *matrona* Cleostrata quickly moves beyond the role of unsympathetic, (quasi-)dowered wife and more closely functions like a Plautine clever slave. The latter, an inventive and mischievous figure typically devises a metatheatrical scheme that allows a young man to enjoy his beloved, most often a prostitute in Plautus, though in extant New Comedy as a whole usually a free person eligible for marriage. The clever slave's dupe may be a universally hated pimp, a foreign soldier or, more transgressively, his elder master and *paterfamilias* (as a source of cash). In *Casina* decorum prevents the freeborn *matrona* from too directly participating in the hoodwinking of Lysidamus, and so Pardalisca and Chalinus carry out deceptive, 'low status' acting roles on Cleostrata's behalf.[46] Still, she unmistakably is the director of *Casina*'s show, and by a remarkable inversion of roles, Lysidamus (not Cleostrata) ultimately is reduced to a slave, fearful for his body and forced to publicly beg his wife for mercy (1000-3). Plautus's complete removal of Euthynicus – as the foolish, but pardonable lover owing to his youth and the possibility of romance – further intensifies the battle between husband and wife and sets the stage for a most compelling marital power struggle. In addition to restraining Lysidamus's moral depravity – as is highlighted in performance by virtually the entire cast's opposition to him in the finale – Cleostrata to her credit also schemes on behalf of Casina, whom we are told in the prologue she regards as a daughter.[47] No clever slave in Plautus is outfitted with such morally sanctioned motives as Cleostrata's, who seems not to be punishing Lysidamus for sheer theatrical pleasure and in the end is not forced to beg forgiveness for her transgressions.

And so, by inversely portraying marriage as a master–slave relationship, what does *Casina* say about the institution of Roman marriage?[48] We could better answer this general question if we were made more certain about Cleostrata's personal motives for acting as she does against Lysidamus. For example, it would be useful to know precisely how she 'realized' (58) her husband was on the prowl for Casina and why she feels 'disdained in the worst way' (189) by Lysidamus – is it simply his disrespect in doing this in plain view, her sense of offended honour, actual jealousy or some combination of motives like these? We perhaps too easily assume that Plautus is not interested in such psychological nuances and doesn't want his audience to be either, or that arranged Roman marriages, real or comic, were necessarily drab, emotionless and purely economic arrangements (cf. pp. 23–8). Cleostrata certainly sounds deeply affected when she pledges wide-ranging revenge against her disgraceful 'lover' (156) of a husband. We perhaps should not automatically preclude consideration of personal feelings from an assessment of Cleostrata's motivations in checking her husband's philandering.

One simple (to us) point that *Casina* seems to make is that a partner's emotions and mutual respect and consideration do count in marriage, and that even if this institution in Rome is asymmetrically structured, both legally and ethically, husbands are not really their wives' masters and so do not possess full licence to treat them tyrannically, that is, like their slaves. Marriage, even in patriarchal Rome, presumably needed to be more like a negotiation and partnership in order to be successful, even if it was not ever fully perceived as a relationship between equals.[49] 'In a general way, the history of [Roman] marriage and the family seems to be characterized by a very slow erosion of the powers of the *paterfamilias*, both as father and husband.'[50] *Casina* thus cleverly demonstrates how marriage is and isn't like slavery. At minimum, the women of *Casina* create a powerful social theatre that disrupts and interrogates traditional notions of authority, gender and sexuality in the course of checking the vicious sexual narcissism of Lysidamus. Cleostrata's return of Lysidamus's cloak and walking-stick (1009), which abruptly follows her call to end the play, obviously signals a return to the domestic status quo. Similarly, the epilogue assumes that husbands like Lysidamus will continue to seek out sex with prostitutes behind their wives' backs (1015–18). From a social perspective, this conservatively ties up domestic matters and shows that the play's extreme inversions of power hold no permanence, though this sudden return to normality cannot erase spectators' experience of seeing how things could be different in a household like that of Lysidamus.

Reception

We are grateful for the survival of one of Plautus's most sophisticated comedies, in no small part because of the many creative adaptations it inspired in the Italian Renaissance and beyond. Playwrights, musicians and screenwriters have found themselves drawn to Plautus's risqué Roman comedy and in it discovered fresh ingredients for their contemporary audiences. While *Casina*'s reception attests to its enduringly humorous and entertaining content, the adaptations also demonstrate how Plautus's sex farce can provide audiences with provocative food for thought.

Transmission, revival and survival to the Renaissance

Modern texts of Plautus's plays are based on two ancient editions: one the fifth-century CE ('Ambrosian') palimpsest, which includes only about half of *Casina*, on which Plautus's plays have been written over by the Book of Kings from the Latin Old Testament (the Vulgate); the other, the so-called 'Palatine recension', which dates to the tenth–eleventh centuries CE. Roman literary scholars began to work critically on texts only in the mid-second century CE, and for a long time many plays circulated under the name of Plautus before a 'canon' of the twenty-one we possess today was eventually established.[1] We remain very much in the dark about the early transmission of Plautus's comedies. Immediately following Plautus's death, his plays probably survived mostly as performances rather than in set scripts/texts. And so whatever modern editors using the rigorous tools of textual criticism hypothesize to be the 'original' script of Plautus's *Casina*, that is, for its premiere sometime around 185 BCE, a printed text of the play today is likely to include alterations, additions and deletions made during the early period of especially fluid transmission. This is verified by *Cas.* 5–20, which were added to an earlier version of the prologue and must belong to a revival performance of *Casina* c. 150 BCE.[2]

These added lines in fact constitute our earliest extant reception of a Plautine play, in so far as the speaker is adapting *Casina*'s prologue to convince his contemporary audience that the play is still worth watching. The speaker of this later prologue argues that, for discerning spectators, an old play is like a fine aged wine for connoisseurs (5–8).[3] This strategy inverts the earlier prologue speaker's emphasis on the need for novelty in plays (see pp. 17–18) and suggests a theatrical milieu in which some spectators are now interested in 'classic' plays. He supports his assertion with an analogy from coin-making ('aren't the new plays today even more worthless than the new coinage', 9–10), as coinage in Rome was often debased. The prologue speaker then dates his insertion of lines (that is, to around the mid-second century BCE) by noting that some of the 'oldsters' (14) in the current audience were around for the first performance, while the 'youngsters' (15) present can't possibly have seen *Casina* (here he subtly anticipates the play's young v. old amorous contest). The speaker, who expresses nostalgia for the previous generation's poets (18–20),[4] claims that *Casina* 'surpassed all plays' (17) when it premiered. Here we rue our ignorance of the competitive aspects of early Roman theatre (and of any accompanying theatrical records) to assess this claim. Plautus's comic reputation presumably is now solid enough that such an assertion, however vague it actually is, might easily meet general approval.

Beyond these lines from the mid-second century BCE revival, we know virtually nothing else of *Casina*'s reception in the ancient

Roman world.[5] Plautine comedy of course remained popular, and there is solid evidence for revival performances down to the end of the Roman Republic.[6] Plautus was also read by elites such as Cicero in the first century BCE, and we know that Plautine comedy enjoyed renewed scholarly attention during the second century CE, owing to interest in archaic literature in a period known as the 'Second Sophistic'.[7] Comedies might have continued to be performed at festival venues and in more private (elite) settings during the empire, but few specifics are known. Aulus Gellius (*Attic Nights*, 1.24.3) preserves a spurious epitaph of Plautus that speaks to the comic playwright's reception among the literate in his day:

> After Plautus's death, Comedy's in mourning.
> The stage is emptied; then Laughter, Play, and Joke
> And all his immeasurable measures lamented together.

Praise of a comedian's humorousness is unsurprising, but the composer of the epitaph cleverly does this through trademark Plautine personifications, including that of 'Play' (*Lusus*), which highlights Plautine comedy's love of metatheatre, as in *Casina*. The epitaph's writer also appropriately emphasizes Plautus's extraordinary musical virtuosity in imagining the ritual mourning of the playwright by his metres. And in describing the stage as empty after Plautus's death, he suggests that Plautine comedy is best seen in live performance.

An acrostic plot summary of *Casina*, probably written in the second century CE, survives (as for all Plautus's plays). The summary represents one reader's perception of the play's most important moments, compressed as these must be into six lines whose first letters vertically spell 'Casina'. The acrostic's composer describes the two slaves as vying for Casina by proxy, but mentions only the interest of Lysidamus and his son (1–2). Mention of Lysidamus's victory in the lottery follows and his subsequent deception (3) is elaborated thus: 'To the old man's detriment, a worthless slave is substituted for the girl, who then roughs up the master and the farm-manager' (4–5). In deeming Chalinus 'worthless', the writer focalizes Lysidamus's perspective of his son's arms-bearer (cf. *Cas.* 257). The acrostic's last line reads, 'The young man marries Casina after she is found out to be a citizen', as though the recognition scene and marriage had taken place during the play, when neither is the case. In what may further be construed as a sympathetic reading of Lysidamus, no mention whatsoever is made of Cleostrata's role or that of the other women who appear in the play! Following this idiosyncratic (mis)reading of the play, we hear nothing definite of *Casina* until the Italian Renaissance. During the Middle Ages, Plautus seems to have yielded to Terence as a Roman comedy text for general use in schools, but Plautus's now canonized plays continued to be copied by hand down to the invention of the printing press.[8]

The sixteenth century (Italy and England)[9]

Casina bursts onto the exciting theatrical scene of the Renaissance in Italy with Girolamo Berrardo's Italian translation into *terza rima*, *Cassina* (1501). While unheralded today as a translation,[10] Berrardo's is the first known adaptation to feature the appearance of Casina and Euthynicus onstage, a move which reorientates its Plautine source toward a typical New Comedy romance. In 1502 Berrardo's translation was performed during the wedding festivities of Lucrezia Borgia and Alfonso d'Este at Ferrara. Under the supervision of Duke Ercole, who lavishly supplied costumes, *Casina* and four other Plautine plays (*Epid., Bac., Mil., As.*) were performed over the course of five days, with Berrardo's *Cassina* (ironically?) being the featured comedy the night of Lucrezia's wedding (her third). Brief but entertaining versions of scenes from these performances can be seen in the television series *The Borgias* (2011–13).[11]

One of the sixteenth century's most intriguing adaptations is Niccolò Machiavelli's (1469–1527) *Clizia*, which was first performed during carnival season in 1525. The prologue speaker jokes about transporting, as Plautus had done, a story set in Athens to Florence in the recent past. Machiavelli basically preserves the stage layout of Roman comedy, with all action taking place within twenty-four hours (in five acts) on a street in front of the house of Nicomaco,[12] a gentleman of Florence, with side wings leading to the marketplace and church. The prologue speaker announces that Clizia, as Casina in Plautus's play, will not appear onstage 'for modesty's sake'. He disingenuously assures spectators that there will be 'no indecency' that will cause ladies in the audience to blush, when in fact *Clizia* is at least as bawdy as its Plautine source.[13] Machiavelli generally follows the plot of *Casina*, sometimes even translating very closely, though he also freely adapts Plautine material for his own purposes.

One of the play's most significant departures is revealed in the opening dialogue between Nicomaco's son Cleandro and a young Florentine friend. Although Nicomaco's wife Sofronia plays a controlling role in *Clizia* commensurate with Cleostrata's, the competition between father and son for the absent Clizia assumes an entirely new centrality. In the opening scene, Cleandro reveals his long-standing love for Clizia, who came to live with the family when she was five. In contrast to Casina, who became Cleostrata's personal charge, Cleandro reports that both his parents 'treated her as their own dear daughter' (1.1). Nicomaco's lust, Casina's unknown origins and her lack of a dowry prevent Cleandro from confessing his love to his parents or seeking marriage with her. As he describes his predicament just before the denouement, 'First I had to contend with my father's passion, now I have to contend with my mother's ambition' (5.5).

Nicomaco and Sofronia have made plans to marry Clizia to their favourite servants, Pirro and Eustachio, respectively. In addition to his losing Clizia, Cleandro fears that his father's fixation on her will lead the old man to divert a considerable portion of his own inheritance to Pirro, in order to ensure the servant's compliance in the sexual proxy scheme (4.1). From the start we witness a family suffering even further disruptions than Lysidamus's. In his monologue immediately following the opening scene, Cleandro likens the lover to a soldier, thus marshalling military imagery that proves to be just as pervasive in *Clizia* as it was in *Casina*, especially in connection with Nicomaco. This becomes most evident in the old man's opening monologue, when he lewdly declares, 'I am not too old yet to break a lance with Clizia' (2.1). Phallic swords, knives and javelins figure prominently in the play.

In their predictably acrimonious first meeting, husband and wife face off regarding Clizia and, as in Plautus (**Scene 4**), Sofronia insists on having a say in Clizia's future, but Nicomaco is adamant that she is his to do with as he pleases. In a monologue, Sofronia clarifies her motivations in not passively accepting her husband's infidelity to an extent not seen in Cleostrata's case: she champions the upper middle-class Florentine family values her husband is defying ('this poor house is going to rack and ruin', 2.4). Nicomaco's infatuation with Clizia over the past year, she maintains, has transformed him from being a decent and serious man to someone who neglects his professional and personal affairs, behaves intemperately and stays out late, and has lost even the respect of the household servants. We again get a more sharply focused view of a house set in chaos than we do in *Casina*.

Cleandro and Nicomaco, who has just learned that his wife has sent for Eustachio, have a tense meeting that ends in the now tyrannical old man's assertion of his masculine authority: 'I intend to be the master in my own house … it is a sad house when the hen crows louder than the cock' (3.1). After Pirro and Nicomaco unceremoniously win the lottery for Casina, Sofronia attempts to delay the wedding by claiming Clizia has 'female monthlies', to which the impatient Nicomaco brutally replies, 'That is nothing some male nightlies won't cure!' (3.7). Like Chalinus in *Casina*, Cleandro overhears his father's plans to use the house he leases to his neighbour Damone for his 'honeymoon' (4.2). Pirro under the cover of night and on some pretext is to vacate the marriage bed for the old man, who pledges to take a male enhancement potion and eat aphrodisiacs of dubious efficacy to ensure that his 'weapon will cock' (4.2). In contrast to Lysidamus, who mostly just emotes like a foolish young man in love, Nicomaco in a more aggressive way seems to be at war with aging and in search of his lost virility.

Cleandro informs his mother of Nicomaco's plans and the women seize control of the comedy by launching their plan to dress one of the servants, Siro, in Clizia's clothes. In imitation of Pardalisca's messenger's speech (**Scene 14**) about Casina, Sofronia's servant Doria tells Nicomaco an enraged Clizia is threatening to kill him and Pirro to avoid the marriage (4.7). Doria next appears to inform the audience of the tricks underway (4.8; cf. *Casina* **Scene 16**) and that the wedding feast is being prepared (there is relatively little development of *Casina*'s food themes in *Clizia*). Nicomaco declares himself 'feeling as lusty as a lance' following his special dinner (4.11). The women deliver Siro to his bridal chamber at Damone's house. To Damone's polite farewell, Sostrata ironically (and ominously) replies, 'You watch out yourselves. You have the weapons, we don't' (4.12).

Doria introduces the final act with her monologue ('I never laughed so hard in my life . . .;' cf. Myrrhina's in *Casina*, **Scene 20**) by announcing that the married women, Cleandro and Eustachio have learned what happened during the night at Damone's (it is now morning). Doria eavesdrops on Nicomaco's detailed confession to Damone. Machiavelli has Nicomaco assume the roles of both Olympio and Lysidamus (**Scenes 21–3**) in recounting the night's experience – a bourgeois Florentine citizen's body apparently was not thought to be as inviolable as a Roman slave owner's. Nicomaco describes a violent struggle with Siro as Clizia. Now openly weeping,

Nicomaco reports that his pleas with the bride-in-disguise met only further violence, followed by Siro's turning onto his belly and clinging to the mattress face down. The frustrated old man then turned away and soon dozed off, only to be forcefully awakened by 'a hard, pointed object' jabbing him just below his tailbone (5.2). In a reprise of Olympio's experience with Chalinus, this led Nicomaco to recall Clizia's fictional knife and he jumped out of bed. Pirro then appeared with a lamp and in Nicomaco's own words, 'instead of Clizia who do I see but Siro, my servant, standing erect all naked on the bed, and out of spite (boo, hoo, hoo!) he was making faces (boo, hoo, hoo!)' (5.2).

Sofronia confronts her weeping husband by pointing out his obvious narcissism ('instead of consoling me as you should be doing, it is I who must console you', 5.3), but quickly displays surprising compassion. She offers to forgive him if he will reassume his previously good character. Fearful of further public disgrace, Nicomaco agrees. We can with some confidence believe that Machiavelli's Nicomaco is capable of reform: 'Nicomaco is isolated and made to see his own folly in a way Lysidamus is not, and is deeply hurt by it.'[14] While unhappily obsessed with Clizia, Nicomaco is nonetheless depicted as far less sexually unrestrained than Lysidamus. Machiavelli's old man strongly denies interest in pederasty when the possibility of having a virgin boy draw in the lottery for Clizia is raised (3.7), nor do we ever see him sexually harassing Pirro as Lysidamus does Olympio. Nicomaco plausibly seems sexually tameable (as he forcibly is at play's end). No obvious gesture signalling a restoration of the marital and familial status quo – equivalent to the return of Lysidamus's cloak and walking-stick – is made at the end of *Clizia*.

Nicomaco further pledges to leave Clizia's affairs to his wife (5.3). Nicomaco and Sofronia then both acknowledge Cleandro's love for Clizia but agree that marriage remains out of the question. Just as Cleandro despairs (5.5), Damone announces the arrival of Ramondo, a nobleman of Naples and Clizia's father, who agrees to the marriage out of gratitude for the family's raising his daughter. With only slightly less abruptness than Plautus's displacement of a New Comedy recognition scene to *Casina*'s epilogue, Ramando fortuitously appears out of thin air like a *deus ex machina* of classical drama. Sofronia is given the play's final words, which suggest she remains securely in control of the household at the end of *Clizia* – more so than Cleostrata at the end of *Casina*. True to her name – Machiavelli makes Sofronia the incarnation of Greek *sōphrosýne*, that is, wisdom, temperance and good judgement – she has used her clever wiles to restore order to the household. Her triumph clearly is an ethical one, even though it is not clear that the power dynamic between Nicomaco and Sofronia has been permanently altered.[15] While in both *Casina* and *Clizia* the female heroine emerges as a sympathetic and controlling figure who rightfully checks her husband's sexual aggression and selfish disruption of familial life, Sofronia more distinctly than her Plautine counterpart is made to enforce social norms and values extending outside the household as well.

Pietro Aretino (1492–1556), a prolific writer and innovative playwright perhaps best known for his sexually explicit sonnets, produced *The Marescalco* or *The Stablemaster* in 1533,[16] a five-act play in Italian that draws extensively from both Plautus's *Casina* and Machiavelli's recent *Clizia*. The Duke of Mantua decides to play a trick on his older bachelor stablemaster by leading his subordinate to believe that he, in order to stay in the Duke's good graces, must marry a young bride. The entire play thus is an elaborate practical joke at the expense of the Marescalco, whose homosexuality and misogynistic tendencies are known within the court. There is no shortage of *Schadenfreude* as the increasingly discomfited Marescalco's fellow courtiers gradually bully him into consenting to the marriage. In Aretino's play the homosexuality of the Marescalco is subtly referred to, usually with quiet tolerance or indifference. The Marescalco's Nurse, while personally sympathetic to him, vaguely urges him to 'leave the ways of shame and sin' and to at last mature through marriage: 'Spruce up your reputation a little. Let go of your youth and start setting up your own house' (1.6).[17] The majority of the comedy's scenes feature characters variously arguing the pros and cons of marriage, as they employ largely conventional set pieces about the institution and women in general to encourage or frighten the Marescalco regarding his apparent fate. As the wedding ceremony concludes, the Marescalco takes a closer look at the bride and is delighted to discover that 'she' is Carlo, the court pageboy (5.10). With no resentment whatsoever, the Marescalco joins in the general laughter at his own expense and the play ends happily with a feast. The noisome Pedant is given *The Marescalco*'s last words in a kind of epilogue (5.12) that promotes misogynist stereotypes and the ill-advisedness of marriage for men.

Despite *The Marescalco*'s being a very different comedy from its Plautine source, some specific elements (in addition to the central bridal substitution) of *Casina* are skilfully remade in Aretino's comedy. As was the case for Plautus's absent Casina, the non-existent bride of *The Marescalco* becomes an imaginative construction of various characters, who invent the bride's status, physical qualities, character attributes and idiosyncratic talents as they describe her to the prospective groom. The Old Woman directly recalls the women of *Casina*'s glee (**Scenes 16, 20**) at their metatheatrical scheming when, with Carlo now dressed for the wedding, she exclaims, 'The most wonderful party in the world! His Excellency has convinced the whole court that he is giving his Marescalco a wife tonight. Now that everyone believes it, he has made us dress up Carlo da Fano as a bride in place of the one everyone thinks he is going to give him' (5.4). The Old Lady and two other women (simply 'Matron' and 'Lady'), who also appear for the first time in this scene, then conduct a final rehearsal for the wedding onstage: Carlo is instructed on how to look and sound demure and, at the request of the Duke himself, must place his tongue in the Marescalco's mouth during the ceremonial kiss.

Other characters in the know soon appear as guests and highlight their status as an internal audience of the 'wedding-show': 'I'd rather go a year without a mass, without a sermon, without vespers than miss such fun as this' (5.6). During the ceremony, the Marescalco reappropriates Lysidamus's semi-coherent joke about splitting himself from sexual excitement[18] by declaring that he is 'ruptured' (5.10), that is, suffering from a hernia, in a last desperate effort to prove himself sexually impotent and so unfit for marriage. Appropriations such as these that virtually invert their Plautine source neatly demonstrate Aretino's creative facility in devising a rich play that ultimately seems to land somewhere in opposition to traditional heterosexual marriage.

We possess another fascinating early adaptation of *Casina* titled *Il Ragazzo* or *The Boy* (1541) by the Venetian humanist and writer Lodovico Dolce (1508–68), who was strongly committed to the translation of Greek and Latin works for a general audience.[19] Dolce's comedy accordingly features the imposture of a young male servant as a young woman to deceive an old man, though it also includes elements of Dolce's own devising (for example, a woman dresses as a man to secretly meet her lover). The target of the main deception, Cesare, is foolishly enamoured of a much younger woman, just as Lysidamus is in *Casina*. Giacchetto, the young and quasi-androgynous servant who is forced by his superior to impersonate the young woman Cesare is in love with, quickly warms to his cross-dressing role. With Plautine-like metatheatricality, Giacchetto is prepared for his role by Ciacco, a parasite who offers extensive training on how to pass as a woman. In sharp contrast to the hyper-masculinized and (probably) weakly disguised Chalinus of *Casina* (see p. 68), Giacchetto makes a beautiful and most convincing young woman (3.2). Giacchetto's onstage rehearsal includes detailed instructions on kissing, and so spectators are treated to a demonstration of various styles of kissing, each (pointedly) somewhere on the chaste/lewd spectrum, between the two men. This consensual eroticism between

Giacchetto and Ciacco makes explicit what remains only implicit and non-actualized in *Casina* because of the honeymoon's violence there, and Dolce's play provides 'a fascinating representation of contemporary perceptions about the gender ambiguity of young males, their sexual danger, and their liminal status'[20] in a way that *Casina* cannot. Cesare's encounter with the disguised lover is reported by Giacchetto (4.1), who tells us that the old man became sexually excited and gropingly discovered his genitals (4.1), thus suffering a shame most similar to Olympio's (**Scene 21**). Dolce, however, has adroitly added the explicit sexual exchange between the men, seemingly for the benefit of a patriarchal culture that viewed such transgression ambiguously, as also cross-dressing, and perhaps to be understood in terms of a citizen's passage to adulthood.[21]

Shakespeare (1564–1616), who most probably read Plautus in Latin and made extensive use of his comedies,[22] utilizes *Casina* in at least two plays, that is, as part of the bard's characteristic appropriation of multiple sources simultaneously. A recent study of *The Comedy of Errors* (1594), whose primary model is Plautus's *Menaechmi*, demonstrates how Shakespeare in Act 2, Scene 1 incorporates thematic and structural elements of *Casina* to alter aspects of *Menaechmi*'s domestic themes in ways that better suit the situation and characters of *The Comedy of Errors*.[23] The character of Luciana, the sister of Adriana (wife of Antipholus of Ephesus) is introduced after the model of Myrrhina in *Casina*. Luciana advocates patient acceptance of her sister's husband's disrespectful behaviour. In her strong sense of rejection and resentment over Antipholus of Ephesus's suspected infidelity, Adriana, like Cleostrata and in contrast to the shrewish Matrona of *Menaechmi*, is thus provided with a friendly confidante in Luciana, which functions to make Adriana a more sympathetic character overall. At the same time, Antipholus of Syracuse's amorous interest in Luciana reconfigures the sexual triangle of *Casina*, and in that he (unknowingly) is pursuing his sister-in-law evokes the incest averted motif of *Casina* (see p. 85); in this way elements of both Myrrhina and Casina are collapsed in the character of Shakespeare's Luciana. Cleostrata, as trickster and punisher of her husband, clearly provides a better model for Adriana than the dowered wife of *Menaechmi*, who is represented as unsympathetic throughout and is put up for auction by her ex-husband at the end of Plautus's play. Adriana in fact emerges victorious in the revenge plot she mounts in the Dr Pinch madness scene (4.4) of *The Comedy of Errors.* Shakespeare's *Merry Wives of Windsor* (c. 1597) similarly has been shown to develop elements of *Casina*, especially the aging Falstaff's Lysidamus-like lechery and the faux-wedding with substitution of a boy, as these have been filtered and (re)processed through the Italian tradition in such plays as Machiavelli's *Clizia*.[24]

The seventeenth century and later

Ben Jonson's (1572–1637) lengthy prose play *Epicene* or *The Silent Woman* (1609) includes an impersonation and faux-wedding plot inspired by both Plautus's *Casina* and Aretino's *The Marescalco*.[25] In *Epicene* young Sir Dauphine Eugenie forges an elaborate plot against his elderly uncle in order to secure his inheritance. The uncle, Morose,[26] is a wealthy misanthrope who despises all noise and so is in search of a 'dumb woman' (1.2.24).[27] Dauphine will be disinherited if the old man marries.[28] Dauphine's scheme is to introduce his disagreeable and tyrannical uncle to a silent woman – in reality a boy he has prepared for this role – with the expectation that their faux-union will end Morose's marriage ambitions once and for all. Though for different reasons from the lascivious men of *Casina*, Morose similarly objectifies the (non-existent) Epicene as his ideal woman, reflecting his own obsession: 'she has brought a wealthy dowry in her silence' (2.5.92–3). The well-trained boy impersonating the young aristocratic woman plays his part well and the marriage plans proceed.

Things begin to turn sour for Morose when the wedding proves to be an especially noisy affair. Morose in anger appears threateningly with a sword and will later wield two swords, as Casina is falsely claimed to be doing by Pardalisca in **Scene 14**. Worst of all, the silent woman quickly morphs into a loud and garrulous wife or 'manifest woman' (3.4.40), as the misogynistic Morose describes Epicene. Morose seeks a divorce and even claims that he is impotent (as the Marescalco had), but this strategy fails because only a wife can initiate divorce on this ground. In the final scene, Dauphine, the mastermind behind all, promises to provide Morose with sure-fire cause to annul the marriage if Morose first signs a contract giving him the inheritance. The old man agrees and Dauphine removes the boy's wig and unveils his scheme: 'you have married a boy: a gentleman's son that I have brought up this half year at my great charges, and for this composition which I now have made with you' (5.4.199–201). The boy thus described is a combination of Casina and Chalinus in relation to the schemer (Dauphine/Cleostrata), who in each play successfully rebels against a socially malignant patriarch. Earlier in the same scene, Jonson nods directly to Plautus when he has Epicene ironically protest about the endangered marriage in a manner similar to Chalinus at the end of *Casina* (1010–11): 'This is such a wrong as never was offered to poor bride before' (5.4.2–3). The final revelation comes as a surprise to the audience and other characters present, but Morose exits in disgrace and this largely asexual play ostensibly reaches a happy ending, though with no marriage.[29]

Casina is a main influence behind Beaumarchais' (1732–99) legendary *Le Mariage de Figaro* (1784), which is considered to be one of the immediate triggers of the French Revolution. In no small part due to its being banned by Louis XVI and subjected to protracted and rigorous censorship before its premiere, *The Marriage of Figaro*, the middle play of a trilogy that includes *The Barber of Seville* (1775) and *The Guilty Mother* (1792), was virtually guaranteed success. The play proved enormously popular, in large part because of Figaro's long monologue that scathingly indicts French aristocratic privilege and abuse of authority (5.3); Napoleon famously called Beaumarchais's comedy 'the Revolution in action'. It likewise enjoyed a vibrant theatrical afterlife via many sequels and adaptations, such as Mozart's comic opera *Le nozze di Figaro* (1786). Because of its perceived dangerously radical ideology, performances of Beaumarchais's *The Marriage of Figaro* were banned by Mussolini in Italy and by the German forces occupying Paris during World War II.

While the plot of *The Marriage of Figaro* is complex and takes various surprise turns, a basic structure similar to that of *Casina* remains visible. Count Almaviva has grown tired of his wife the Countess, and demands sexual 'privileges' from Suzanne, the Countess's chambermaid, who is engaged to Figaro (the Count's valet and steward of the castle in Agas-Frescas), who in the manner of a clever Plautine slave had engineered the intrigue that resulted in the Count's marriage with the Countess (then Rosine) in *The Barber of Seville*. In *The Marriage of Figaro* a series of plots involving impersonation and costuming in connection with Figaro's and Suzanne's wedding evolves, which culminate in a successful ruse devised and executed by the main female characters. The Count is frustrated in his attempt to sexually exploit Suzanne and compelled to seek forgiveness from his wife in the end.

In the play's opening we meet the main pair of young lovers, Figaro and Suzanne, who in contrast to Plautus's Euthynicus and Casina not only occupy the stage for much of the action but participate in the intrigue against the play's patriarch threatening their romance. The opening scene is set in a bedroom near the Count's that he suspiciously has designated for the newlyweds (it is the morning of their wedding). Even more suspiciously, the Count has just reintroduced the *droit du seigneur* (an archaic practice symbolic of a feudal lord's oppression) that he had banned when he married the Countess. Suzanne is fully aware of the Count's intentions and characterizes him to Figaro as a habitual adulterer: 'Count Almaviva is tired of chasing all the pretty women in the locality' (1.1), and instead of returning home to his wife he now desires Suzanne in this honeymoon suite.[30] Seemingly in imitation of *Casina*, Figaro initially devises a plan to dress Chérubin, an impulsive, androgynous and highly sexualized pageboy, in Suzanne's clothes to entrap the Count during the evening's marriage celebrations.[31] Figaro has troubles of his own to address, as Marceline, an older housekeeper, is in love with him and hopes to use a legal claim to force Figaro to marry her instead of Suzanne. The Count out of self-interest rules in Marceline's favour, but before matters can proceed any further, in a delightful parody of classical recognition scenes (3.16) Figaro displays a birthmark on his arm that reveals he is Marceline's son (incest averted!). Suzanne pays off Marceline's claim with money from the Countess and the Count is left angry and frustrated.

The Countess, after learning of her husband's plans from Suzanne, has in the meantime assumed an active, Cleostrata-like role in advancing the young lovers' cause (and her own) by rejecting Figaro's plan to dress Chérubin as Suzanne, and instead proposes to impersonate Suzanne herself this coming evening (2.24). Figaro, the expected mastermind in any plot against the Count, is thus effectively cast aside, and ultimately must deal with his own unwarranted jealousy concerning Suzanne. The two women now assume the theatrically powerful role of tricksters and seize control of the play. Suzanne deceptively agrees to meet the Count beneath some chestnut trees in the estate's gardens, on the condition that he allows her to marry Figaro and provides a dowry.

The Count meets up with the Countess dressed as Suzanne in what can be interpreted as a brilliant recasting of *Casina*, **Scene 19**, in which Lysidamus and Olympio, now in possession of their bride, persist in imagining Chalinus to be a delicate and tender Casina (see pp. 89–91). The Countess says little when the two meet in the darkness, but imitates Suzanne's voice successfully when she speaks, as the Count alternately fantasizes about Suzanne's body (in reality his wife's) and opines about marriage at length:

> Such skin! So soft, so silky! The Countess's hand isn't half as smooth to the touch! ... Or her arms as firm, as shapely. Or her fingers as pretty and elegant and teasing ... The fact is, Suzanne, I've often thought that if husbands look outside of marriage for their pleasures which they don't find inside it, it's because wives don't think enough about how to keep our love alive, how to renew theirs, how to – what's the word? – renovate its pleasures by varying them.
>
> 5.7

As Suzanne and Figaro eavesdrop and comment in asides, the Count divulges his feelings about his marriage to his wife and then gives the Countess the money he agreed to give Suzanne, along with a diamond, in anticipation of a sexual encounter.

The Countess ultimately reveals herself and the discomfited Count begs forgiveness from her, and he is compelled to forgive all the courtiers involved in the intrigues (5.19). The Countess hands over the money and diamond to the newlywed lovers, and all loose ends seemingly are tied up. Figaro gets the last word (before a final song), jesting with the audience as Plautine characters sometimes do at play's end: 'Wife and wealth apart, I should be truly honoured and very happy if you would be [my friend].' But it is the women who manifestly triumph here, even if we assume a return to the marital status quo and the Count's reversion to serial adultery – and we need not. The Count has been punished and publicly shamed for abusing his authority in his attempt to sexually misuse a subordinate and denigrate her husband. The other remarkable speech of *The Marriage of Figaro* (in addition to Figaro's rant about aristocratic abuse) is Marceline's about men's virtual enslavement of poor women through economic and sexual exploitation (3.16), which provides another explicit example of how Beaumarchais has transformed a comedy of character and intrigue into one of ideas.[32] Among the various issues of class contentiousness, privilege and power raised by *The Marriage of Figaro* is the emancipation of women. Beaumarchais's adaptation of *Casina* for a markedly different socio-political milieu and at a very different moment of history brashly and brilliantly releases the latently subversive potential of Plautus's sex farce.

Plot elements of *Casina, Curculio, Pseudolus* and *Miles Gloriosus*, along with bits from other Plautine comedies, are combined to create *A Funny Thing Happened on the Way to the Forum* (lyrics by Stephen Sondheim, script by Larry Gelbart and Burt Shevelove), which premiered on Broadway in 1962 and spawned the 1966 Richard Lester film.[33] The film (starring Zero Mostel as Pseudolus), which has aptly been described as 'Jewish-American humor [meeting] the classics' and a transference of 'Rome into Brooklyn',[34] features pervasive punning, double-entendres, repetition jokes, deft employment of irony and characters speaking at cross-purposes, neologisms and other verbal and physical comedy that would please Plautus himself. *Casina* is tapped for the film's cross-dressing scene, in which the male slave Hysterium impersonates the beautiful young Philia in a bridal costume as unconvincing as we assume Chalinus's was in an effort to keep Captain Miles Gloriosus from taking her away from Hero, the silly young man in love with her. As Pseudolus prepares Hysterium for his role, he encourages his diffident charge by pretending to find him sexually irresistible and the pair perform a delightful reprise of Philia's song 'Lovely'. The film's married couple, Hero's parents Senex and Domina, distil the writers' interpretation of Cleostrata and Lysidamus. Senex, in sharp contrast to *Casina*'s Lysidamus, is represented as a sort of 'loveable old scamp' as he constantly jokes at his wife's expense and the film generally focalizes his misogynistic views of women and marriage.[35] Domina stereotypically is presented as a humourless, henpecking wife,[36] who owing to Pseudolus's presence is stripped of her clever and creative role in *Casina* (and is even made to lust after the braggart Captain!). Domina's song 'That Dirty Old Man' attempts to lend some complexity to her character in that it shows her expressing both the truculence of Cleostrata's first song in *Casina* (**Scene 2**) and wounded feelings at her husband's constant sexual straying: 'That dirty old man divine! / I loathe him, / I love him, / That lecherous, lewd, lascivious, loathsome, lying, lazy / Dirty old man of mine!' But to a reader of *Casina* coming to the modern film, *A Funny Thing Happened on the Way to the Forum* seems markedly more sexist (*mutatis mutandis*) than its Plautine source. Apart from Domina as 'the battle-axe wife', the women of the film include the pretty, but intellectually feckless Philia ('Lovely' I'm lovely, / All I am is lovely. / Lovely is the one thing I can do . . .') and the repeatedly specularized prostitutes in Lycus's brothel next door. In one protracted scene the latter are made the locus of assorted male fantasies (stripping, ménage à trois, subjection to a dominatrix) that reflect a 1960s American sexual revolution seemingly for men only.[37]

No other modern film that I am aware of mobilizes elements of *Casina* so overtly as *A Funny Thing Happened on the Way to the Forum*, although hundreds of films, such as *Some Like it Hot* (1959), *The Rocky Horror Picture Show* (1975) and *White Chicks* (2004), combine deception, intrigue and cross-dressing to explore themes of sexuality and gender. A pervasive trope in American television sit-coms is the smart, at times transgressive wife who is forced to outwit her obtuse, loutish and sometimes lecherous husband, from Ralph Cramden to Homer Simpson, in order to preserve familial values and restore some semblance of domestic harmony. We perhaps should not expect to see a close adaptation of *Casina* during a historical epoch such as ours, in which cross-dressing, same-sex marriage and transgendering are growing more socially (and legally) acceptable.

The various adaptations described in this chapter nonetheless highlight Casina's most appealing and enduring dialectical features, as they also reciprocally offer fresh insights into Plautus's ancient Roman comedy. Along with Aristophanes' cross-dressing and women-on-top comedies (*Lysistrata, Women at the Thesmophoria, Assemblywomen*), *Casina* remains one of Western drama's foundational texts through which to fruitfully approach always evolving notions of gender, sex, interpersonal power and marriage.

APPENDIX

The Structure of *Casina*

SCENES	LINES	CHARACTERS
Prologue	1–88	
Scene 1	89–143	(Olympio, Chalinus)
Scene 2	144–64	(Cleostrata, Pardalisca)
Scene 3	165–216	(Myrrhina, Cleostrata)
Scene 4	217–78	(Lysidamus, Cleostrata)
Scene 5	279–308	(Lysidamus, Chalinus)
Scene 6	309–52	(Olympio, Lysidamus)
Scene 7	353–423	(Cleostrata, Chalinus, Lysidamus, Olympio)
Scene 8	424–36	(Chalinus)
Scene 9	437–514	(Olympio, Lysidamus, Chalinus)
Scene 10	515–30	(Lysidamus, Alcesimus)
Scene 11	531–62	(Cleostrata, Alcesimus)
Scene 12	563–90	(Lysidamus, Cleostrata)
Scene 13	591–620	(Alcesimus, Lysidamus)
Scene 14	621–719	(Pardalisca, Lysidamus)
Scene 15	720–58	(Olympio, Chytrio, Lysidamus)
Scene 16	759–79	(Pardalisca)
Scene 17	780–97	(Lysidamus, Pardalisca)
Scene 18	798–814	(Olympio, Lysidamus)
Scene 19	815–54	(Pardalisca, Olympio, Lysidamus, Cleostrata, Chalinus)
Scene 20	855–74	(Myrrhina, Pardalisca, Cleostrata)

Scene 21	875–936	(Olympio, Cleostrata, Pardalisca, Myrrhina)
Scene 22	937–62	(Lysidamus, Chalinus, Olympio, Cleostrata, Pardalisca, Myrrhina)
Scene 23	963–1011	(Chalinus, Lysidamus, Cleostrata, Myrrhina, Pardalisca, Olympio)
Epilogue	1012–18	

Simplified metrical outline of *Casina*

A = spoken iambics, B = sung mixed metres, C = 'recitative' trochaics (for 'ABC succession', see Moore (2012: 253–5); for musical arcs, see pp. 7–8)

ARC 1	A: 1–143	(Prologue, Scene 1)
	B: 144–251	(Scene 2–Scene 4, 251)
	C: 252–308	(Scene 4, 252–Scene 5)
ARC 2	A: 309–52	(Scene 6)
	C: 353–423	(Scene 7)
ARC 3	A: 424–514	(Scenes 8–9)
	C: 515–62	(Scenes 10–11)
ARC 4	A: 563–620	(Scenes 12–13)
	B: 621–758	(Scenes 14–15)
ARC 5	A: 759–97	(Scenes 16–17)
	B: 798–846	(Scene 18–Scene 19, 846)
ARC 6	A: 847–54	(Scene 19, 847–54)
	B: 855–962	(Scenes 20–2)
	C: 963–1018	(Scene 23, Epilogue)

Notes

Chapter 1

1   An index of *Casina*'s scenes, lines and characters can be found in the Appendix.
2   Gratwick (1973: 8).
3   Germany (2016: 147).
4   For *Casina* I most closely follow the Latin text of Questa (2001); all translations are my own (some are adapted from Christenson (2015)).
5   The prologue speaker's assertion in this context that Plautus has written Diphilus's source play 'anew in Latin' (33–4) reflects a seasoned playwright's confidence in translation across theatrical traditions as a creative, adaptive process: see pp. 10–13. Connors (2004: 182) sees further irony in the punning name: 'the echo of *latine* ['in Latin'] in the sound of the word for "barking" (*latranti*) seems to suggest that Latin itself might be a kind of barbarous barking'.
6   For Atellan farce, see pp. 4–5.
7   For Plautus's adaptation of Greek New Comedy models, see pp. 10–18.
8   The earliest known Latin writers were fluent in Greek, Latin and some dialect of southern Italy (see Feeney (2016: 66–9)). The claim of Plautus's Umbrian birth is disputed, as it may only be an extrapolation from a real-estate pun on *umbra*, 'shade', and Umbria: 'if you don't have shade, is there at least a [shady] lady from Sarsina?' (*Mos.* 770).
9   These include epic and lyric poetry, in addition to tragedy and comedy (Christenson (forthcoming (b))).
10 For this enterprise, see Goldberg (2005).
11 Cf. Gratwick (1982: 808–9).
12 For the Artists of Dionysus, see p. 7. For constructions of Plautus's life, see Fontaine (2014: 533–4).
13 For the beginnings of Latin literature, see Feeney (2005).
14 Cf. Most (2003: 388): 'The Romans recognized themselves from the beginning as latecomers in the highly competitive market-place of the

Hellenistic Mediterranean, and seem to have decided early that a program of intense translation was the best strategy for catching up: given that it was the Greeks who dominated that market-place, it was inevitable that it was to Greek literature that the Romans should from the very beginning have primarily oriented their translating activity. In the absence of a Ministry of Culture, the decisions involved were individual, unsystematic and largely the work of poets.'

15 For the Roman translation project, see McElduff (2013) and Feeney (2016).

16 For Latin intertextuality in general, see Hinds 1998; the case for reading Plautus intertextually is made by Sharrock (2009: 18–21, 201–19).

17 Overviews of Atellan farce include Beare (1964: 137–48) and Panayotakis (2005).

18 Cf. also, in Greek myth, the marriage of Herakles and Omphale, which featured gender role-reversal with cross-dressing. During their honeymoon, Herakles (still in women's garb) violently rebuffed Pan for attempting to rape him (cf. Ov. *Fast.* 2.303–59 and **Scenes 21–3** of *Casina*).

19 For sketches of the genre, see Fantham (1989), Beare (1964: 149–58) and Panayotakis (2005: 139–46). Illustrations of Roman imperial mime can be found in Dunbabin (2016: 114–37).

20 For overviews of Greek New Comedy, see Lowe (2007: 63–80) and Ireland (2010).

21 See further the study of Lape (2004).

22 Webster (1970: 172–5).

23 An account of the diffusion of Greek New Comedy can be found in Nervegna (2013).

24 Useful overviews of the *palliata* include Gratwick (1982), Manuwald (2011: 144–56) and Lowe (2007: 81–96).

25 These include trochaics (possibly chanted) and *cantica* or fully integrated songs in a mix of metres. A piper (*tibicen*) was always onstage, either playing or poised to do so: see Moore (2012: 27–35).

26 Marshall (2006: 203–25).

27 For the musical arcs of *Casina*, see Appendix.

28 For specific festivals in Plautus's day, see Franko (2014).

29 See further Brown (2002).

30 For this *choragus* in Plautus, see *Cur.* 464–86, *Pers.* 159–60, *Trin.* 857–60.

31 Plautus's plays typically require four to six speaking parts (plus mute characters and a piper): see Marshall (2006: 83–125).

32 Elite Romans derided actors for displaying their bodies in public for entertainment purposes (not unlike prostitutes) and so counted them among the 'publicly disgraced' (*infames*): see further Edwards (1993).

33 Manuwald (2011: 55–68).

34 Cf. Gruen (1992: 209): 'The ritual of erecting and then dismantling temporary structures gave annual notice that the ruling class held decisive authority in the artistic sphere.'

35 For functional differences between Greek and Roman theatrical spaces, see Wiles (1991: 36–67).

36 Goldberg (1998).

37 Moore (1994).

38 For masks in Plautus, see Wiles (1991: 129–49) and Marshall (2006: 126–58). For costumes, see Duckworth (1952: 88–94), Wiles (1991: 188–208) and Marshall (2006: 56–66). We do not know if costumes featured phalluses (as in Roman mime; cf. Marshall (2006: 62–4)); if they did, we might expect some euphemistic references to these in Plautus.

39 For the function of props in Plautus, see Marshall (2006: 66–72).

40 On the conventions and effects of eavesdropping in Plautus, see Slater (1985: 11–12, 162–5) and Moore (1998: 34–40).

41 For text and translation of *Dis Exapaton*, see Handley (1997) and Arnott (1979). The bibliography on the parallel texts is vast, but insightful analyses include Bain (1979), Anderson (1993: 3–29), Handley (2001) and Fontaine (2014: 519–26).

42 *Bac.* 229, 521–3, 530–2, 703–4.

43 See *Bac.* 362, 687, 1183a.

44 Parmeno or 'Trusty' is a common slave's name in Greek comedy.

45 1912: 131.

46 Thus Fontaine (2014: 526).

47 For 'transformation and identification motifs' in Plautus, see Fraenkel (2007: 17–44).

48 Virtually all Plautus's characters have purely Greek names: see Fontaine (2010: 63, 253–6 and passim).

49 Gratwick (1982: 113). Characters even use hybrid words, as when Myrrhina employs a neologism, *dismarite*, 974 (Greek *dis*, 'twice', + Latin *maritus*, 'husband'), in pointing to Lysidamus's failed attempt to make Casina his concubine.

50 For a translator's (in)visibility, see Venuti (2008).

51 See p. 7. A similarly metapoetic moment occurs at the end of Plautus's *Pseudolus* (191 BCE), when the eponymous clever slave during a very Plautine song and dance performance that probably replaces a wedding in Plautus's Menandrean source (Christenson (forthcoming(b))) soils his *pallium*: 'Plautus is, jokingly, telling us what he does with Greek plays – he messes them up. This is a comic-programmatic way of saying that he alters them, puts in Roman bits, spoils them: makes his own plays out of the material ... Plautus uses Pseudolus, then, to celebrate his own position in the tradition of comedy' (Sharrock (1996: 173)). Cf. also Leigh (2000: 300): 'every time a character refers to "my *pallium*" he is also drawing attention to his theatrical costume, to the marker of the burlesque national identity which he has embraced'. Cf. Rei (1998: 103).

52 Lysidamus here coins a Latin verb, *expalliatus sum*.

53 As also Olympio's loss of his cloak (934).

54 Barbiero (forthcoming) similarly sees Plautus's emphasis on 'newness' in *Casina* as a kind of provocation to spectators to consider larger programmatic issues: 'we should read the various claims to novelty throughout the Plautine corpus also in the context of this cultural enterprise [translation]; that is, as Plautus's awareness of his pioneering role in the new history of Latin literature'.

55 See *Cas.* 118, 782, 798, 815, 859, 881, 892, 1011.

56 Unless they know Diphilus's play and that it contained a same-sex marriage between slaves (this is unclear). This presumably would constitute a minority of spectators.

57 Such as the elimination of Euthynicus as a character (see pp. 37–8).

Chapter 2

1 For an overview of the wars of this period, see Gargalo (2010).

2 For the expanded Roman social system, see Alföldy (1988: 29–41).

3 For Plautine comedy's cultural and historical contexts, see Gruen (1990: 124–57) and Leigh (2004).

4 'Plautus does not wear his heart on his sleeve. But he exhibits a keen sensitivity to the issues of his time and the dispositions of his contemporaries' (Gruen (1990: 157)).

5 For contemporary debates about the spoils of war and related issues of conquest in Plautus, see Gruen (1990: 133–7).

6 For the Plautine clever slave's frequent appropriation of such aristocratic posturing, see Leigh (2004: 47–56).

7 *armiger* ('arms-bearer', 55).

8 See 307, 344, 629, 660, 691, 706, 749, 909–10 and pp. 59–62, 91.

9 *uirtute uera*, 88; '*uirtus* ... does not mean courage simply, but stands rather for the whole aristocratic ideal with its emphasis on *gloria* won by the commission of great deeds in the service of the *respublica* according to certain standards of conduct' (Earl (1960: 238)). The prologue speaker's valediction here (87–8) provides no indication of a specific military conflict. The language is very similar to *Cist.* 197–8, whose context clearly reveals that these lines were written during the Second Punic War (*c.* 209–207 BCE: de Melo (2011b: 129–30)).

10 Plautine characters use 'barbarian' to mean 'Roman' as they ironically assume the attitude of culturally superior Greeks. See pp. 22–3, 64–5.

11 Cf. Gruen (1990: 157): 'The dramatist's ear is attuned to public attitudes and sensibilities: to Greek impressions of Romans and Romans' of Greeks, to the heady welcome of Greek culture in Rome and the corresponding uneasiness and resistance to it.'

12 Livy 1.13.3. The story also demonstrates how women might also serve as intermediaries between their natal and marital families (Skinner (2005: 201–2)).

13 As articulated by a character at Pl. *Capt.* 889.

14 Dixon (1992: 72). Insightful accounts of Roman marriage include Rawson (1986: 1–57) and Dixon (1992: 61–97). For legal

matters related to marriage, see Gardner (1986: 31–56) and Treggiari (1991).

15 Saller (1994: 102–32).

16 There are only young and old men in New Comedy. While 'old age' was a fairly fluid concept in the Roman world (Parkin (2003: 149–59)), comic *senes* like Lysidamus may be assumed to be at least sixty.

17 For the legalities of concubinage, see Treggiari (1991: 51–2) and Gardner (1986: 56–60).

18 Lysidamus also juxtaposes *cum Casina* and *cubet/cubitet* (with reference to his wife, 483–6); this running verbal play is rounded off by Chalinus as he pursues Lysidamus at 977 *imus cubitum? Casina sum* ('Are we going to bed? I'm Casina').

19 A series of puns with the root *cub-*, found in both the Latin word for 'elbow' (*cubitum*) and 'bed' (*cubitus*; cf. the verb *cubito*, 'lie down/have sex'), highlights this development: 849, 853, 901, 923, 965, 977.

20 A woman in a *sine manu* arrangement thus (functionally) remains a daughter within her father's family and so could initiate a divorce (Watson (1967: 48, 54); Treggiari (1991: 443–4)), as Alcmena seems to do at *Am.* 928.

21 Dixon (1992: 74–6).

22 Thus Watson (1967: 29–31) and Rei (1998: 101–2). Dees (1991) makes a case for Cleostrata being in a *sine manu* marriage.

23 Myrrhina's response, 'Strange, if true: it's usually the men who want more "rights" from their wives' (191–2), puts a sexual spin (that is, 'conjugal rights') on Cleostrata's remark about her legal rights and reflects her tendency to look at marriage from a traditional (male) perspective in this scene.

24 Strong (2016: 32).

25 Gardner (1986: 105–6); Treggiari (1991: 350–6).

26 The value of dowries, at least among elite women, seems to have increased greatly during the Second Punic War: see Evans (1991: 53–83). For legal developments related to the dowry during this period, see further Saller (1994: 207–24).

27 Women of the lower classes might work outside the home in shops linked to their husbands' trades, or they worked, of necessity, in

low-status businesses such as inns and taverns. See further Evans (1991: 101–65).

28 Evans (1991: 27–33).

29 Cf. Livy's claim (22.55.1–8) that, as rumours of Hannibal's approach reached the city, Roman women took to streets and created public disturbances. Cf. also Livy 27.50.5.

30 Beard, North and Price (1998: 82).

31 Livy 34.1.3. Culham (1982) argues that the *Lex Oppia* was a conservative response to women's increased public visibility in religious activities during the war with Hannibal.

32 '[The Oppian Law's] principal value was symbolic rather than pragmatic. The appearance of women, bedecked and bejeweled, in public would be offensive at a time of economic hardship and national crisis. This *lex* imposed a patriotic uniformity' (Gruen (1990: 144)).

33 An insightful account of the debate can be found in Agati Madeira (2004).

34 For dating the play, see Maclennan and Stockert (2016: 23–4); for detailed analysis of Megadorus's speech, see Christenson (2014: 23–30).

35 Cf. the similar impersonation of a dowered wife at *Mil.* 687–9 and 692–8 by the old bachelor Periplectomemus.

36 See pp. 25–8. Lysidamus later concedes that Cleostrata has a 'right' (371) to determine Casina's fate; this of course is not an admission that Cleostrata owns the girl, but a husband's politic acknowledgement that his wife deserves some input in the matter (and Lysidamus's acknowledgement of the point here makes the lottery possible).

37 See further Johnston (1980). For the dating of *Poen.* to *c.* 189 BCE, see de Melo (2012: 13–14).

38 Livy 39.8–19. Livy (25.1.6–12) also records an earlier attempt to control women's religious practice during the Hannibalic war, possibly in connection with the cult of Bacchus (see Beard, North and Price (1998: 91–2)).

39 'The campaign against [Bacchic worship] had a larger meaning for the senate as an institution. The Bacchanalian affair became a vehicle to assert the collective ascendency of the institution, to claim new

prerogatives in the judicial sphere, in the regulation of worship, and in the extension of authority in Italy' (Gruen (1990: 78)).

40 In Lysidamus's utterly inept attempt at gaining sympathy, he perhaps means to suggest a (mythic) scenario like that of Euripides' *Bacchae*, where the voyeuristic Pentheus is torn apart by Maenads for infiltrating their ritual (Rei (1998: 103–4)).

41 There is also a metatheatrical dimension to Myrrhina's words here: 'With her theatrical double entendre, *ludunt*, Myrrhina reminds Lysidamus that the women have gained power over the performance: their play, not a performance with bacchants, is now being performed' (Moore (1998: 178)).

42 The suggestion that Lysidamus is the real Bacchant here might especially have resonated with Plautus's audience owing to sensational reports that women in the cult forced male worshippers to engage in sex with each other (MacCary (1975b)). Slater (1985: 93) comments, 'Lysidamus's lust is not human, not a straying within the limits that society and comedy can tolerate, but animalistic, frenzied, Bacchic.'

Chapter 3

1 As is the case for several Plautine plays (the alternatives of having either a character in the play or a divine speaker deliver the prologue were established in Greek New Comedy).

2 Marshall (2006: 195–6).

3 For the layout of the theatre, see pp. 9–10.

4 The *senex* is never called Lysidamus in the play, but the name appears in the scene headings of the Ambrosian palimpsest (see p. 101). The name is historically attested in Athens: MacCary and Willcock (1976: 95–6). Possible etymologies include 'Freer of the people' (Greek *lusis* + *dēmos*) or 'Divorcer of spouse' (*lusis* + *damar*): cf. López López (1991: 120–1). Alcesimus's name seems to mean 'Helper/Defender' (cf. Greek *alkē*), a moniker he decidedly proves not to live up to.

5 For the thesis that an actor playing Fides delivers the prologue, see, most recently, Connors (2016).

6   Cf. Williams (1993: 34).

7   As will become clear, disgrace and public shame (*flagitium*) fast accrue to Lysidamus in this comedy: 155, 160, 552, 876, 937, 991.

8   *Sortientes* (not *Casina*) may have been Plautus's title: cf. *Merc.* 9–10 and MacCary and Willcock (1976: 102).

9   Cf. Plautus's *Asinaria* and *Mercator* (and Petrone (2007)).

10 The Lysidamus of the play, a deeply flawed master/*paterfamilias*, typically does not act so decisively: see pp. 47–9, 61–3.

11 The prologue speaker's insistence that Euthynicus 'won't come back to town in this comedy today' (64–5) strongly suggests that he appeared in Diphilus's play (O'Bryhim (1989: 82–3)).

12 The name (first used at 134) incongruously suggests Zeus' cult-centre at Olympia, famed for its athletic contests, as well as Mount Olympus, the home of the gods. For the motifs of Lysidamus as Jupiter and the erotic competition for Casina, see pp. 49, 65, 87.

13 Roman slaves did, however, form long-term relationships without legal sanction, as *contubernales*, lit. 'tent-sharers' (cf. *Mil.* 181). Cf. Dixon (1992: 90–1) and Treggiari (1991: 52–4).

14 Unless they know Diphilus's play and it contained a same-sex marriage between slaves (this is unclear). This presumably would constitute a minority of spectators.

15 Mercury, the prologue speaker of Plautus's *Amphitruo* (a unique example of a *tragicomoedia* or 'mythical travesty' in Roman comedy) uses a similarly specious strategy (Christenson (2000: 156) to acclimate spectators to the prospect of Jupiter appearing as a character in the play: 'as if something new were being presented in Jupiter's becoming an actor' (89–90).

16 See pp. 67–70. Cody (1976) and Konstan (2014) argue that the homoerotic elements, and perhaps the substitution of same-sex for heterosexual marriage, are the main innovations of *Casina*.

17 That is, she will not be subjected to the sexual violence the male characters desire: see pp. 85–7.

18 Or they were at least assumed to do so because of their profession and stigmatization as *infames*: Edwards (1993: 123–31).

19 Cf. the verb *sequi*, 'to follow', at 91, 92 and 94.

20 For a city slave/country slave 'type scene' in Plautus, cf. the strongly
   moralizing exchange of Grumio and Tranio, *Mos.* 1–83.

21 For this typical refrain of Plautus's clever slaves (*lubet*), see Leadbeater
   (1986) and Richlin (2017: 233–7).

22 In not making Chalinus urbane here, Plautus is preparing us for his
   incongruous role as a bride (i.e. the delicate sixteen-year-old imagined
   by Lysidamus and Olympio). Chalinus is unusually dubbed Euthynicus's
   squire (*armigerum*, 55), and likely is to be played as tough, aggressive
   and physically, though not necessarily mentally, imposing: Anderson
   (1983).

23 Olympio ironically (cf. **Scene 21**) has Casina use a word for 'sparrow'
   with phallic associations (Adams (1982: 31)).

24 From the scant evidence for Roman comedy's so-called 'recitative'
   trochaic septenarii, Moore (2012: 92–104) concludes that their mode of
   delivery fell somewhere between our notions of speaking and singing
   (and so was not uniformly 'recitative', as is often assumed).

25 Female characters (of various statuses) are given the first song in eight
   Plautine plays, perhaps reflecting an audience preference for such
   performances by skilled male actors (Moore (2012: 87–90, 246)).

26 Tobias (1980). For what little can be gleaned about how actors might
   have imitated women's singing voices, see Moore (2012: 87–90).

27 Rei (1998: 102).

28 Moore (1998: 168).

29 Her name (revealed in 170–1) means, somewhat incongruously for her
   character, 'Myrtle', a sweet-smelling herb with sexual associations in
   Greek comedy. The fact that she bears the same name as the neighbour
   of the heroine of Aristophanes' *Lysistrata* is suggestive. In that comedy a
   salacious and boozy Myrrhine serves as a sharp foil to the high-minded
   Lysistrata ('Dissolver of the Army', reflecting the play's successful 'sex
   strike'), who like Cleostrata protests against male misbehaviour and
   devises a punitive scheme. Bilingual spectators with extensive
   knowledge of Greek comedy might draw a connection between the two
   plays and anticipate Cleostrata's ultimate heroism in humiliating her
   husband. It is unlikely that Plautus has simply transliterated the names
   of Diphilus's characters: see p. 11.

30 Moore (2012: 126–7).

31 The expression of such an emotion can be suggested by movements and
    gestures in masked comedy. For aspects of their 'female speech', see
    Dutsch (2008: 31–2).

32 For a detailed analysis of the less deferential language the women use in
    this scene once they're assured no one is listening, see James (2015:
    110–11).

33 In other words, a mere speech act, as discussed by Rosenmeyer (1995),
    who also reviews the (contested) evidence for whether or not Roman
    women could initiate divorce in this way.

34 Spectators can easily imagine that further conversation has occurred
    offstage when the women next appear together (see p. 70). Critics
    generally have overstressed the apparent inconsistency in Myrrhina's
    opposition to Cleostrata here and her later complicity in humiliating
    Lysidamus. Feltovich (2015a) argues convincingly that Myrrhina
    consistently acts as a loyal friend in *Casina*, and in this scene is only
    looking out for what she perceives to be her friend's best interests. In
    this light, Plautus has masterfully created a naturalistic, dialectical scene
    between two women contemplating a proper course of action (such
    collaboration in Plautus more typically takes place between slaves,
    sisters or unmarried females, not *matronae*: Fantham (2015 92); cf.
    Feltovich (2015b)). Given contemporary controversies (see pp. 28–32),
    spectators probably found the discussion here interesting and a source
    of dramatic tension, especially in the suggestion that any effort to
    punish the *paterfamilias* potentially bears serious consequences.

35 From the start, Lysidamus absorbs all our attention (not unlike a petulant
    and narcissistic young child): 'the personality of Lysidamus is the key to
    the play's action. The rest of the players react to his character; indeed they
    exist as characters chiefly in reaction to him' (Tatum (1983: 87)).

36 Cf. Corbeill (1996: 163–4).

37 For Roman moralists, a man's use of prostitutes became problematic
    when it grew expensive; cf. the famous anecdote about Cato the Elder,
    who after seeing a friend exit the same brothel several times, tells the
    man: 'I praised you because I thought you were a visitor here, not a
    resident' (scholiast on Hor. *Sat.* 1.2.31–5).

38 For the tragic parody here, see Chiarini (1978: 109).

39 This ironically becomes true when Olympio later (see p. 71) attempts to rape Casina before Lysidamus, the play's Jupiter, can exercise *droit du seigneur*.

40 The use of such militaristic language by Lysidamus (cf. 357 and see pp. 21–2) only underscores that he has no strategy here, apart from winning the (chance) lottery.

41 Roman comedy features many of these 'ensemble scenes'; for the thesis that Cleostrata has been added for Plautus's version of the urn scene of the Greek original, see Franko (2004: 42, 46). Her presence visually signifies the true nature of the contest.

42 For the means by which actors establish and maintain focus in Plautus, see Marshall (2006: 160–74).

43 Cf. Slater (1985: 78): 'The scene offers us a striking picture, with Cleostrata at the apex of a visual triangle of power: she holds the urn centre stage, while Lysidamus and Chalinus hover nervously on either side of her.'

44 Interpreting his command *aequa*, 'equalize (the lots)', as technical language for the shaking of the lots (thus *OLD aequo* 8b and MacCary and Willcock (1976: 144)).

45 For *Casina*'s pronounced emphasis on the potential for forced sexual labour, see Marshall (2015).

46 We learn nothing of the nature of Euthynicus' desire for Casina, apart from its mirroring his father's (48–9). His passion is at least age-appropriate, and we are spared seeing him manifest anything like Lysidamus's monstrous lust.

47 Euripides' *Aeolus* featured a marriage lottery that resulted in the tragic suicide of Canace (cf. Ov. *Ep.* 11).

48 For verbal dexterity as a typical tool in a slave's arsenal, see Stewart (2012: 173–6).

49 For the normality of such jokes by slaves in Plautus and in a society where they regularly were subjected to sexual assault by their masters, see Williams (2010: 36–8). The social sanctioning of the master's sexual prerogative does not make such violent acts non-traumatizing for the victims, and the seeming casualness with which they joke about these

may be (naturalistically) viewed as an affective response to their brutalization.

50 Segal (1987: 25); cf. Beacham (1992: 100). For a master's 'localization and containment of violence in the body of the slave', an extension of Varro's notorious description of a slave as a 'tool with a voice' (*instrumentum uocale*), see Way (2000).

51 For examples of these in Plautus, see Fontaine (2010: 37–89).

52 Petrone (1983: 91–2).

53 Cf. Chalinus's report in his monologue following the lottery: 'how nervous he was, the way the wretch fretted about' (432).

54 Cf. Chalinus's subsequent description, 'how he jumped up and down after the farm-manager won' (433).

55 Spoken in iambics and marking the start of a new musical arc. The cessation of music here, immediately following the intense spectacle of the lottery (and Chalinus's defeat), marks a new seriousness of purpose.

56 Duckworth (1952: 116–17).

57 Marshall (2006: 141 n. 64). He thus appropriately positions himself to take revenge against Olympio for his earlier sadistic fantasy of Chalinus's entrapment inside the bedroom wall (see pp. 40–2).

58 'In Plautus eavesdroppers take on a function of the now-vanished chorus [of Greek drama] – to comment on, and guide the audience's response to, what they overhear. The eavesdroppers function in effect as an onstage audience' (Slater (1987: 7)).

59 Richlin (2017: 106) points out that the word for bladder here can be used of the vagina in Latin sexual slang (and so Chalinus's barb further effeminizes Olympio).

60 'Today' (*hodie*) in Plautus typically means 'in the play' (Dunsch (2016: 130–2)).

61 'Cleostrata and her allies, including Chalinus, repeatedly overhear the monologues and asides of their opponents, Lysidamus and Olympio, and this ability to eavesdrop successfully will help considerably in aligning Cleostrata's side with the spectators' (Moore (1998: 168)).

62 See further Christenson (forthcoming (a)).

63 Cf. Weissinger (1940: 86) and Marshall (2006: 176–81).

64 Lysidamus here childishly mimics objections to his behaviour ('with your grey hair', 'at an inappropriate age', 518) that recall Cleostrata's at 239.

65 We may presume she has been brought up to speed by Chalinus offstage (the empty stage at the end of **Scene 10** supports passage of time for this).

66 As though she were a comic parasite at a feast (MacCary and Willcock (1976: 161)).

67 Cf. Slater (1985: 84): 'she is now the exultant gamester and plotter'.

68 Plautus has him comment on the artifice of the convention of asides: 'she'd have to be deaf not to have heard this' (575).

69 Comedy generally loves repetition: for this particular device in Plautus, see Sharrock (2009: 175–8).

70 She is first named at 631. Plautus (see p. 11) has given her a name especially appropriate for this scene, as the panther in the ancient world was believed to possess an alluring breath with which it attracted its prey (Connors (1997: 306–7)).

71 For the maid's stereotypical 'discourse of pain' in Plautus, see Dutsch (2008: 118–24).

72 Williams (1993: 50–1) devises extensive stage directions for how this might be played.

73 Cf. *As*. 668–9.

74 She easily draws Lysidamus into an echo chamber of anxiety, e.g. Lys. 'What was the uproar inside?' Par. 'Your maid began something awful inside . . .'. Par. 'Inside, your maid is . . .'. Lys. 'What's she up to inside?' (649–56).

75 Cf. Lysidamus's description of his wife as 'a bad thing' (*mala res*, 228) and Anderson (1993: 104–5).

76 Their exchange largely repeats that of Cleostrata and Lysidamus after his first slip (see p. 51).

77 Chytrio has only two brief utterances: for such 'walk-on' roles in Plautus, see Marshall (2006: 100–1).

78 Cf. *Ps*. 702 ('I'll address the man in grand style'), where Pseudolus proceeds to speak both paratragically and in Greek.

79 Cf. Slater (1985: 86): 'Olympio has done nothing to deserve such exalted status: he has displayed none of the cleverness that is the basis for such comic superiority'.

80 See *TLL* 1.0.1890.61–6.

81 For Greek *pragma* as a euphemism for the male sexual organ in Aristophanes, see Henderson (1991: 116). The use of Greek is not always 'low class' in Plautus, as is often claimed: Jocelyn (1999). Adams (2003: 354–5 n. 105) observes that the evidence of Plautus suggests that 'code-switching was polarized at the two social extremes [of upper and lower class]'.

82 The Greek *mega kakon* here is a back translation of the Latin *malum magnum*, 'a great beating'.

83 See further Gowers (1993: 53–107).

84 A Plautine mannerism in monologues: Fraenkel (2007: 5–16).

85 See p. 7. The *tibicen*, while always conspicuous onstage, is not usually engaged by the actors (Moore (2012: 27–35)).

86 Pardalisca plays the role of a *pronuba*, the married (free) woman who led Roman brides to the bridal chamber (Cleostrata has her slave carry out this deceptive role for her in the faux-wedding here).

87 Casinus is a masculinization of Casina, here addressed only to the women by Pardalisca.

88 Treggiari (1991: 163).

89 Marshall (2006: 60).

90 See further Williams (1958), who identifies both Greek and Roman elements in *Casina*'s ceremony.

91 Cf. Cat. 61.162–4.

92 See further MacCary and Willcock (1976: 190).

93 Amid all the farce, the song broaches serious themes related to power and property in Roman marriage: cf. Pardalisca's mention of the husband's financial responsibilities (821–2) and see pp. 25–8.

94 That is, marriage is a speech-act (in a legitimate wedding between free persons a *matrona* fulfilled this function).

95 For the 'right of first night' and related cross-cultural rituals, see MacCary (1975a).

96 Cf. Dutsch (2015: 24): 'the men are too wedded to the mental image of a delicate girl and to the exterior appearance of "the bride" to draw rational conclusions'.

97 Moore (2012: 177) notes that Plautus often marks the onset of spoken iambics with a character's command for silence.

98   Andrews (2004) analyses the play's (and women's) use of indoor/
     outdoor space in detail.

99   She recalls her instructions to the bride (**Scene 19**); *moriger*, 'obedient',
     is a traditional ideal of Roman marriage (Williams (1958: 98)).

100 Philippides (2015) argues that Pardalisca's mention of a radish (911)
     suggests *raphanidosis*, an ancient punishment of adulterers via anal
     insertion of a radish.

101 His essentially naked appearance emblematizes his public disgrace
     and complete lack of self-control as a *paterfamilias*: Letessier (2014:
     71–2).

102 Cf. Cody (1976: 461).

103 Marshall (2006: 110); cf. Franko (2004: 47). Cf. Moore (1998: 177):
     'Staging underscores the fact that Lysidamus has reached his nadir, for
     he is overheard now by no fewer than five eavesdroppers.'

104 Chalinus's unusually brash behaviour toward his master, in addition to
     being the result of Lysidamus's impotence, may be explicable in terms
     of his possible status as a 'dowry slave' who came with Cleostrata to the
     marriage and remains her property (Rei (1998: 97)). For Roman actors'
     possible use of falsetto, see Christenson (2000: 43).

105 Cf. *OLD subigo* 4 for the idea 'tame', 'dominate'.

106 *Merc.* 203–4, *Mil.* 652, 1402.

107 Cf. Fantham (2015: 103).

108 This may visually suggest Hercules' use of his club. The frightened
     Lysidamus shortly characterizes the walking-stick as such (967, 971),
     which he fears – in yet another phallic struggle – will be used to
     emasculate him ('he'll depilate my loins', 968).

109 The juxtaposition of Cleostrata's formal and respectful style of
     greeting ('I bid you greetings') with her sardonic address here is richly
     ironic.

110 Beacham (1992: 114).

111 In Olympio's claim that his reputation has been stained by Lysidamus's
     'disgraceful acts' (*flagitiis suis*, 991), Suárez (2007) sees a reference to
     flagitatio, an Italian form of folk justice through public shaming.

112 For the distinctively Roman legalistic solution here, cf. the contract
     struck in the epilogue of *Merc.* (1015–26).

113 Cf. Forehand (1973: 249), who notes that 'Olympio's response to his predicament is much more like the reaction of a decent Roman *senex*, whereas Lysidamus is acting like a guilty slave.'

114 Cf. Fitzgerald (2000): 85–6.

115 Dutsch (2008: 152) notes that Cleostrata here defies the misogynistic stereotype of women ignoring time constraints.

116 For a convenient overview of the issues, see Sharrock (2009: 250–8).

117 Cf. Marshall (2006: 196–7).

118 For the 'work' of Plautine epilogues, see Slater (1985: 153–4) and Christenson (2016).

119 *Cas.* ultimately effects the expected marriage between free persons, but Plautus significantly relegates this to a few lines of the prologue and epilogue. For the general suppression of marriage and romance in Plautus, see Wiles (1989).

120 *scortum* (1017; cf. 1019) is the most pejorative term for a prostitute in Latin (Adams (1983: 321–7)).

121 For the incongruity of goatish smells and eroticism in (humorous) Roman poetry, see Petrone (2014).

Chapter 4

1 Overviews of Roman sexuality include Skinner (2005: 192–239), Dixon (2001: 32–44) and Ormand (2009: 128–45).

2 See further Williams (2010: 17–29) and Parker (1997).

3 Cf. Chiarini (1978: 113). For *stuprum* generally, see Williams (2010: 103–22).

4 Williams (2010: 84–93).

5 Treggiari (1991: 299–319).

6 Cf. *Menaechmi* 790–802, where a *paterfamilias* defends the double standard to his unhappily married daughter.

7 Treggiari (1991: 229–61), Dixon (1992: 83–9), Williams (2010: 50–9).

8 According to the conventions of New Comedy, the lovesick young man's predicament is fixable, whether through marriage (even if he has raped the betrothed) or the exclusive purchase or long-term rental of a

prostitute (Plautus's preferred resolution overall). Cf. Ormand (2009: 147–9).

9 Cf. also the 'he-goat soaked in sewage' of the epilogue and its suggestions of Lysidamus.

10 Corbeill (1996: 128–73).

11 Chalinus's hirsute body cannot be romanticized like a youth's (see p. 82). Forehand (1973: 244) comments that 'the old man is a lecher, pure and simple, without redeeming virtues'. Cf. Lysidamus's extreme, quasi-sexual identification with Olympio as they are about to receive the bride Chalinus: 'my comrade, my partner, my co-husband' (797), taken as evidence of 'a homiosocial bond between master and slave' by Gold (1998: 25).

12 MacCary and Willcock (1976: 35–6) (after Northrop Frye) see 'a comic Oedipal situation' in the play.

13 These include having Alcesimus empty his house of all possible witnesses, free and slave, for the old man's planned tryst with Casina (521–7).

14 For the idea of excessive desire passing over into illness in Roman thought, see Williams (2010: 200).

15 For the sexual sense of the Latin verb *dirrumpo* ('to burst apart'), see Adams (1982: 150–1).

16 'Lysidamus' cane, a marker of his age and authority, becomes in turn a sword and a club, (weapons aimed both at himself and others) and a phallus' (Gold (1998: 24)).

17 Andrews (2004: 461).

18 For example, Ormand (2009: 149) writes of a slave-boy's monologue about the sexual perils he faces at Plautus's *Pseudolus* 767–88 thus: 'the Roman audience could only think of him as a sexual object and would never have to squirm at the uncomfortable thought of identifying with him'. For a contrary view of the boy's disturbingly personal and compellingly delivered monologue, see Christenson (forthcoming (b)). For the thesis that Plautine comedy sometimes spoke to the concerns of the marginalized in the audience, see now Richlin (2017).

19 A similar moment occurs in the prologue of Plautus's *Captives*: 'this performance is real for us, a play for you' (52), with Moore (1998: 195–6).

20 Cf. Segal (1987: 25), who sweepingly claims, 'Plautine wives are nothing but a parade of untamed shrews', and includes Cleostrata and *Casina* in his discussion of plays that illustrate this stereotype.

21 As an indication of her commitment to women's traditional household roles, Myrrhina announces that she seeks Cleostrata's company because weaving by herself makes her sleepy (168–9), i.e. potentially less productive.

22 Cleostrata of course can also be seen conforming to wifely expectations, for example, when she dutifully follows Lysidamus's orders to make wedding preparations after Olympio wins the lottery (418–21) and when she claims supervision of the maids as her domestic responsibility (261), though she usually does so with some alternate purpose in view (i.e. she is 'acting').

23 Some – not universally accepted as reliable – ancient sources include the theft of keys (especially if these provide access to alcohol), along with adultery, as legitimate grounds for a husband to put to death (or simply divorce) his wife: Evans (1991: 10–11), Moore (1998: 168).

24 Fantham (2015: 92) argues that it is the philandering Plautine husband's sexual frailties that lead to his demise: 'what puts wives in control of the action is their husbands' guilt, as in *Casina*'.

25 Dutsch (2008: 78–9) notes that the lovestruck Lysidamus's coaxing speech effeminizes him.

26 For the likelihood that the name is Plautus's invention and not taken over from Diphilus, see p. 11.

27 Cf. Gold (1998: 23).

28 Cf. Andrews (2004: 449): 'Her identity changes and evolves according to the intent and gender of the character creating an image of her or directing her actions so that the audience must gradually formulate and re-shape an identity for her as the comic action unfolds.'

29 See p. 69. Chalinus's representation of the teenage Casina is so unrealistic that he 'never really [becomes] a specularized female body for the audience' (Gold (1998: 25)), as often does happen in cross-dressing performances (see pp. 111–12). For the hypothetical ways in which Roman male spectators might nonetheless sexually identify with the various male characters here, see Gold (1998: 21).

30 In *Casina* this role is subtly co-opted by Cleostrata: see pp. 96–9.

31 Connors (1997: 305) describes the full range of cinnamon's uses as a perfume, condiment and medicine in the ancient world.

32 For Roman notions of the 'coldness' of old age, see Cokayne (2003: 38–41).

33 She angrily dubs him *Accheruntis pabulum*, lit. 'fodder for the Underworld'.

34 Of Lysidamus's mention of spice as a metaphor for love in 219, MacCary and Willcock (1976: 126) write, 'one has a strong suspicion that somewhere here (or in 225; cf. also 814), there is an allusion to *casia* "cinnamon"'.

35 'Sex, for the *senex*, is better than food, and the love of Casina ... is a *condimentum* rather than the meat and potatoes of his diet' (Franko (1999: 6)).

36 McCarthy (2000: 107) comments that 'Since food in this play has represented control and the satisfaction of desires, conceding his dinner until tomorrow is tantamount to conceding his authority.'

37 By a kind of feast or famine comic logic here, when the men are denied their meal and Casina, the two married women are awarded their food (decorum prevents their claim to any sexual triumph).

38 See Richlin (2017: 127) for the use of hunger to control Roman slaves.

39 See Connors (1997: 306–7) and pp. 59–63.

40 Cody (1976: 457) examines the language of this scene and concludes that 'the homosexual approaches of Lysidamus are presented by Plautus as a dish that Olympio finds disgusting'. Cf. Tatum (1983: 87): 'The spice and fragrance of women, symbolized by such names as Casina (cinnamon) and Myrrhina (myrrh), find a counterimage in the stench of Lysidamus's body and his breath.' A character equates foul breath with an empty stomach at *Mer.* 574.

41 Cf. Aristophanes, *Lysistrata* 663–6, where the men's half-chorus strips and declares, 'A man should smell like a man.'

42 Christenson (forthcoming (a)) and Gowers (1993: 78–93).

43 'Cleostrata's revenge depends partly on a borrowed phallus' (Gold (1998: 26)).

44 Cf. Moore (1998: 179): 'the inversion of the expected roles of men and women has gone on far enough, and the real issue of the marriage relationship is not to be dealt with in a comedy'.

45 An excellent summary of Casina's role and sexual reversals can be found in Slater (1985: 92–3).

46 Cf. Rei (1998: 102): 'Cleostrata is shown to be hampered by a lack of legal avenues that justifies her recourse to a slave's ruse.'

47 James (2015: 113) stresses Cleostrata's maternal feelings as a main motivating factor in the play.

48 I have benefitted much from the insightful and complex argument of McCarthy (2000: 77–121) on this point, though I reach different conclusions from hers here, and do not start from the necessary assumption that it is 'doubtful that Plautus intended to express any social critique' (80).

49 Cf. McCarthy (2000: 101): 'Cleustrata's theater does not seek to create new realities by fiat but rather emphasizes the irreducible necessity for negotiation, that is, that seemingly passive subordinates (wives, slaves, the audience) can block or twist the effect of the desires of the authoritative.'

50 Dixon (1992: 77).

Chapter 5

1 Probably by Varro: *Vidularia*, the last play alphabetically, is virtually lost. For a brief history of Plautine comedy's transmission, see Tarrant (1983); for the manuscript tradition of *Casina* in particular, see MacCary and Willcock (1976: 233–5) and Questa (2001). Aulus Gellius (*Attic Nights*, 3.1.11) counted 130 plays still circulating as Plautus's in the second century CE.

2 For a vigorous defence of this date for a first period of Plautine revival, see Mattingly (1960).

3 Lit., 'those who are smart' (*sapientis*, 5); the speaker's choice of verb recalls *Casina*'s food themes, as the Latin verb *sapio* means both 'to taste' and 'to have taste/be smart'. Chalinus puns on the word's double senses

at 494 (as he is eavesdropping on Lysidamus's request for wedding feast items), as does Lysidamus at 780.

4   Perhaps again riffing on *Casina*'s culinary themes, the speaker rounds off his bit here by referring to this prior generation as 'the bloom of poets' (*flos poetarum*, 18); cf. the 'bouquet' of the aged wine at the opening of his addition to the prologue.

5   For examples of Plautine reception in later Roman authors, in comedy and other genres, see Ferri (2014).

6   Manuwald (2011: 108–19).

7   Aulus Gellius and Apuleius belong to this movement.

8   Bishop (2001) finds traces of Roman comedy in Chaucer's (late fourteenth-century) *Canterbury Tales*, including specific elements of *Casina*.

9   For a comprehensive list of early modern to contemporary performances of *Casina*, see the University of Oxford's Archive of Performances of Greek and Roman Drama (APGRD) database: http://www.apgrd.ox.ac.uk/productions/canonical-plays/casina/180.

10 Hardin (2018: 82) characterizes *Cassina* as 'padded' ('Thus 24 scenes and 1,018 lines become 32 scenes and 3,500 dreary verses').

11 Season 1, episode 4.

12 The character's name may playfully recall that of Machiavelli, who at the time of *Clizia* was engaged in an affair with a much younger singer.

13 All translations of *Clizia* are from the bilingual edition of Sices and Atkinson (1985).

14 Braybrook (2001: 4).

15 For gender issues in the play (and Machiavelli's thought), see further Spackman (2010).

16 *The Marescalco* was written for the Gonzaga court of Mantua in 1526 and later published during Aretino's exile in Venice. The stablemaster's proper name is never given, as is the case for various other characters designated only by type in the play.

17 All translations of *The Marescalco* are from Sbrocchi and Campbell (1992). The Nurse offers the play's meanest judgement on the Marescalco's sexuality when (to another character) she speaks of his 'nasty pleasures' as worthy of harsh punishment and hopes that his

example will encourage men like him to marry (2.4). An actor, by choosing to adopt or avoid gay stereotypes in playing the Marescalco, can of course greatly influence the reception of this aspect of his character.

18 *Cas.* 810 and see p. 67.

19 For his career, see Terpening (1997).

20 Giannetti Ruggiero (2005: 752).

21 Cf. the Nurse's thoughts on the Marescalco's development (see pp. 109–10) and Giannetti Ruggiero (2005: 760). There is also some crossover here with elite Roman male views of sexuality: see pp. 81–2.

22 Duckworth (1952: 412–18).

23 Traill (2011), who writes of her approach: 'I am not claiming that these transformations are all author-directed, much less that Shakespeare had in mind any conscious or deliberate project of translation. It was inevitable that Plautine elements that were dramaturgically viable in a different cultural context would reappear in a culturally more relevant guise' (521).

24 See further Miola (1993).

25 For Jonson's extensive use of Roman comedy in his plays, see Duckworth (1952: 418–23).

26 The uncle's character type is taken from the fourth-century CE Greek rhetorician Libanius's *Sixth Declamation* (Duckworth (1952: 421)).

27 The numeration of *Epicene*'s text here is Dutton's (2003).

28 Morose is referred to as a Latin *senex* at 2.6.12.

29 For themes of sexuality and gender in *Epicene*, see Dutton (2003: 88–96).

30 All translations of *The Marriage of Figaro* are from Coward (2003).

31 While this plan never comes to fruition, Chérubin, who is at odds with the Count and has been banished from the castle, is twice disguised in women's clothing to escape detection and in the finale is dressed as a military officer.

32 This is the central argument of an excellent study of the play by Howarth (1995: 157–95).

33 For the many stage performances of A *Funny Thing Happened on the Way to the Forum* continuing to this day, see the APGRD database: http://www.apgrd.ox.ac.uk/productions/scripts/7765.

34 Malamud (2001: 34).

35 Senex joins the other male principals in the song 'Everybody Ought to have a Maid'; here we find ourselves in the fraternal world of Henny Youngman and his one-liner, 'Take my wife ... please.'

36 One of the most influential studies of Plautus to appear in this era, Segal (1987) (the first edition was published in 1968), in its at times simplistic schematics reduces Cleostrata to 'the bitchy wife' (23). For a thorough critique of Plautus's wives as necessarily the unsympathetic spoilers of their husbands' due pleasure, see Kraus (2004).

37 Cf. Malamud (2001: 39).

Guide to Further Reading and Works Cited

Manuwald (2011) provides a broad overview of Roman Republican theatre, both comic and tragic. The most useful general introductions to Roman comedy are Duckworth (1952) and Gratwick (1982). Petrides (2014) critiques major trends in modern scholarship on Plautus. Gruen (2014) and Leigh (2004) examine Plautine comedy against its contemporary social-historical background. For Plautus's stagecraft, Marshall (2006) is indispensable, as is Moore (2012) for Plautine metre and music. Among the best studies of *Casina* as a play in performance are Slater (1985: 70–93) and Moore (1998: 158–80). The analysis of Beacham (1992: 86–116) draws on the author's experience staging *Casina*. Fitzgerald (2000: 81–6) and McCarthy (2000: 77–121) offer stimulating studies of *Casina* in terms of Roman master–slave relationships. The 1976 commentary of MacCary and Willcock remains an insightful guide to those reading the play in Latin. Tatum (1983) provides a lively translation of *Casina* for performance, while de Melo (2011b) (with facing Latin text) and Christenson (2015) (with notes) produce closer renderings of Plautus's text.

Works cited

Adams, J. N. (1982), *The Latin Sexual Vocabulary*, Baltimore, MD: Johns Hopkins University Press.

Adams, J. N. (1983), 'Words for "Prostitute" in Latin', *Rheinisches Museum für Philologie*, 126: 321–58.

Adams, J. N. (2003), *Bilingualism in the Latin Language*, Cambridge: Cambridge University Press.

Agati Madeira, E. M. (2004), 'La *lex Oppia* et la condition juridique de la femme dans la Rome républicaine', *Revue internationale des droits de l'antiquite*, 51: 87–99.

Alföldy, G. (1988), *The Social History of Rome*, trans. D. Braund and F. Pollock, Baltimore, MD: Johns Hopkins University Press.

Anderson, W. S. (1983), 'Chalinus *armiger* in Plautus' *Casina*', *Illinois Classical Studies*, 8: 11–21.

Anderson, W. S. (1993), *Barbarian Play: Plautus' Roman Comedy*, Toronto: University of Toronto Press.

Andrews, N. E. (2004), 'Tragic Re-presentation and the Semantics of Space in Plautus' *Casina*', *Mnemosyne*, 57: 446–64.

Arnott, W. G. (1979), *Menander*, Vol. I, Cambridge, MA: Harvard University Press.

Bain, D. (1979), 'Plautus *vortit barbare*: Plautus, *Bacchides* 526–61 and Menander, *Dis Exapaton* 102–12', in D. West and T. Woodman (eds), *Creative Imitation and Latin Literature*, 17–34, Cambridge: Cambridge University Press.

Barbiero, E. (forthcoming), 'What's New? The Possibilities of Novelty in Plautus' *Casina*', in C. Demetriou and S. Papaioannou (eds), *Plautus doctus*, Madison: University of Wisconsin Press.

Beacham, R. C. (1992), *The Roman Theatre and its Audience*, Cambridge, MA: Harvard University Press.

Beard, M., North, J. and Price, S. (1998), *Religions of Rome, Vol. 1: A History*, Cambridge: Cambridge University Press.

Beare, W. (1964), *The Roman Stage*, London: Methuen.

Bishop, K. A. (2001), 'The Influence of Plautus and Latin Elegiac Comedy on Chaucer's Fabliaux', *Chaucer Review*, 35: 294–317.

Braybrook, J. (2001), 'Remy Belleau's *La Reconnue* and Niccolò Machiavelli's *Clizia*', *Renaissance Studies*, 15: 1–16.

Brown, P. G. McC. (2002), 'Actors and Actor-managers at Rome in the Time of Plautus and Terence', in P. Easterling and E. Hall (eds), *Greek and Roman Actors: Aspects of an Ancient Profession*, 225–38, Cambridge: Cambridge University Press.

Chiarini, G. (1978), 'Casina o della metamorfosi', *Latomus*, 37: 105–20.

Christenson, D. (2000), *Plautus: Amphitruo*, Cambridge: Cambridge University Press.

Christenson, D. (2014), 'A Roman Treasure: Religion, Marriage, Metatheatre, and Concord in *Aulularia*', in I. N. Perysinakis and E. Karakasis (eds),

Plautine Trends: Studies in Plautine Comedy and its Reception, 13–42, Berlin: de Gruyter.

Christenson, D. (2015), *Hysterical Laughter: Four Ancient Comedies about Women*, Oxford and New York: Oxford University Press.

Christenson, D. (2016), 'All's Well That Ends Well? Old Fools, Morality, and Epilogues in Plautus', in S. Frangoulidis, S. J. Harrison and G. Manuwald (eds), *Roman Drama and its Contexts*, 215–29, Berlin: de Gruyter.

Christenson, D. (forthcoming (a)), '*nouo modo nouom aliquid inuentum*: Plautine Priorities', in D. Dutsch and G. F. Franko (eds), *A Companion to Plautus*, Malden, MA: Wiley-Blackwell.

Christenson, D. (forthcoming (b)), *Plautus: Pseudolus*, Cambridge: Cambridge University Press.

Cody, J. M. (1976), 'The "Senex Amator" in Plautus' *Casina*', *Hermes*, 104: 453–76.

Cokayne, K. (2003), *Experiencing Old Age in Ancient Rome*, London and New York: Psychology Press.

Connors, C. (1997), 'Scents and Sensibility in Plautus' *Casina*', *Classical Quarterly*, 47: 305–9.

Connors, C. (2004), 'Monkey Business: Imitation, Authenticity, and Identity from Pithekoussai to Plautus', *Classical Antiquity*, 23: 179–207.

Connors, C. (2016), 'Nothing to do with *Fides*? The Speaker of the Prologue and the Reproduction of Citizenship in Plautus' *Casina*', in S. Frangoulidis, S. J. Harrison and G. Manuwald (eds), *Roman Drama and its Contexts*, 215–29, Berlin: de Gruyter.

Corbeill, A. (1996), *Controlling Laughter: Political Humor in the Late Roman Republic*, Princeton, NJ: Princeton University Press.

Coward, D. (2003), *Beaumarchais: The Figaro Trilogy*, Oxford and New York: Oxford University Press.

Culham, P. (1982), 'The *Lex Oppia*', *Latomus*, 41: 786–93.

Dees, R. L. (1991), 'Aspects of the Roman Law of Marriage in Plautus' *Casina*', *Iura: rivista internazionale di diritto romano e antico*, 39: 107–20.

de Melo, W. (2011a), *Plautus: Amphitryon, The Comedy of Asses, The Pot of Gold, The Two Bacchises, The Captives*, Cambridge, MA: Harvard University Press.

de Melo, W. (2011b), *Plautus: Casina, The Casket Comedy, Curculio, Epidicus, The Two Menaechmuses*, Cambridge, MA: Harvard University Press.

de Melo, W. (2012), *Plautus: The Little Carthaginian, Pseudolus, The Rope*, Cambridge, MA: Harvard University Press.

Dixon, S. (1992), *The Roman Family*, Baltimore, MD: Johns Hopkins University Press.

Dixon, S. (2001), *Reading Roman Women: Sources, Genres and Real Life*, London: Duckworth.

Duckworth, G. E. (1952), *The Nature of Roman Comedy*, Princeton, NJ: Princeton University Press.

Dunbabin, K. M. D. (2016), *Theater and Spectacle in the Art of the Roman Empire*, Ithaca, NY: Cornell University Press.

Dunsch, B. (2016), 'Sat habeo, si cras fero: zur dramatischen, Funktion der temporalen Deixis bei Plautus, Terenz und Menander', *Würzburger Jahrbücher für die Alterumswissenschaft*, 29: 123–50.

Dutsch, D. (2008), *Feminine Discourses in Roman Comedy*, Oxford: Oxford University Press.

Dutsch, D. (2015), 'Feats of Flesh: The Female Body on the Plautine Stage', in D. Dutsch, S. James and D. Konstan (eds), *Women in Roman Republican Drama*, 17–36, Madison: University of Wisconsin Press.

Dutton, R. (2003), *Epicene, or The Silent Woman: Ben Jonson*, Manchester and New York: Manchester University Press.

Earl, D. (1960), *The Moral and Political Tradition of Rome*, Ithaca, NY: Cornell University Press.

Edwards, C. (1993), *The Politics of Immorality in Ancient Rome*, Cambridge: Cambridge University Press.

Evans, J. K. (1991), *War, Women and Children in Ancient Rome*, London: Routledge.

Fantham, E. (1989), 'Mime: The Missing Link in Roman Literary History', *Classical World*, 82: 153–63.

Fantham, E. (2015), 'Women in Control', in D. Dutsch, S. James and D. Konstan (eds), *Women in Roman Republican Drama*, 91–107, Madison: University of Wisconsin Press.

Feeney, D. (2005), 'The Beginnings of a Literature in Latin', *Journal of Roman Studies*, 95: 226–40.

Feeney, D. (2016), *Beyond Greek: The Beginnings of Latin Literature*, Cambridge, MA: Harvard University Press.

Feltovich, A. (2015a), 'In Defense of Myrrhina: Friendship between Women in Plautus' *Casina*', *Helios*, 42: 245–66.

Feltovich, A. (2015b), 'The Many Shapes of Sisterhood in Roman Comedy', in D. Dutsch, S. James and D. Konstan (eds), *Women in Roman Republican Drama*, 128–54, Madison: University of Wisconsin Press.

Ferri, R. (2014), 'The Reception of Plautus in Antiquity', in M. Fontaine and A. C. Scafuro (eds), *The Oxford Handbook of Greek and Roman Comedy*, 767–81, Oxford: Oxford University Press.

Fitzgerald, W. (2000), *Slavery and the Roman Literary Imagination*, Cambridge: Cambridge University Press.

Fontaine, M. (2010), *Funny Words in Plautine Comedy*, Oxford: Oxford University Press.

Fontaine, M. (2014), 'Between Two Paradigms: Plautus', in M. Fontaine and A. C. Scafuro (eds), *The Oxford Handbook of Greek and Roman Comedy*, 516–37, Oxford: Oxford University Press.

Forehand, E. (1973), 'Plautus' *Casina*: An Explication', *Arethusa*, 6: 233–56.

Fraenkel, E. (2007), *Plautine Elements in Plautus*, trans. T. Drevikovsky and F. Muecke, Oxford: Oxford University Press.

Franko, G. F. (1999), 'Imagery and Names in Plautus' *Casina*', *Classical Journal*, 95: 1–17.

Franko, G. F. (2004), 'Ensemble Scenes in Plautus', *American Journal of Philology*, 125: 27–59.

Franko, G. F. (2014), 'Festivals, Producers, Theatrical Spaces, and Records', in M. Fontaine and A. C. Scafuro (eds), *The Oxford Handbook of Greek and Roman Comedy*, 409–23, Oxford: Oxford University Press.

Gardner, J. F. (1986), *Women in Roman Law and Society*, London and Sydney: Croom Helm.

Gargalo, D. J. (2010), 'The Mediterranean Empire (264–134)', in N. Rosenstein and R. Morstein-Marx (eds), *A Companion to the Roman Republic*, 147–66, Malden, MA: Wiley-Blackwell.

Germany, R. (2016), *Mimetic Contagion: Art and Artifice in Terence's Eunuch*, Oxford: Oxford University Press.

Giannetti Ruggiero, L. (2005), 'When Male Characters Pass as Women: Theatrical Play and Social Practice in the Italian Renaissance', *Sixteenth Century Journal*, 36: 743–60.

Gold, B. (1998), '"Vested Interests" in Plautus' *Casina*: Cross-dressing in Roman Comedy', *Helios*, 25: 17–29.

Goldberg, S. (1998), 'Plautus on the Palatine', *Journal of Roman Studies*, 88: 1–20.

Goldberg, S. (2005), *Constructing Literature in the Roman Republic*, Cambridge: Cambridge University Press.

Gowers E. (1993), *The Loaded Table: Representations of Food in Roman Literature*, Oxford: Oxford University Press.

Gratwick, A. S. (1973), 'Titus Maccius Plautus', *Classical Quarterly*, 23: 78–84.

Gratwick, A. S. (1982), 'Drama', in E. J. Kenney and W. V. Clausen (eds), *Cambridge History of Latin Literature*, Vol. II, 77–137, Cambridge: Cambridge University Press.

Gruen, E. (1990), *Studies in Greek Culture and Roman Policy*, Berkeley: University of California Press.

Gruen, E. (1992), *Culture and National Identity in Republican Rome*, Ithaca, NY: Cornell University Press.

Gruen, E. (2014), 'Roman Comedy and the Social Scene', in M. Fontaine and A. C. Scafuro (eds), *The Oxford Handbook of Greek and Roman Comedy*, 601–14, Oxford: Oxford University Press.

Handley, E. (1997), 'Menander: *Dis Exapaton*', *The Oxyrhyncus Papyri*, 64: 14–42.

Handley, E. (2001), '*Actoris opera*: Words, Action and Acting in *Dis Exapaton* and *Bacchides*', in R. Raffaelli and A. Tontini (eds), *Lecturae Plautinae Sarsinates IV*: *Bacchides*, 13–36, Urbino: QuattroVenti.

Hardin, R. F. (2018), *Plautus and the English Renaissance of Comedy*, Madison and Teaneck, NJ: Fairleigh Dickinson University Press.

Henderson J. (1991), *The Maculate Muse: Obscene Language in Attic Comedy*, 2nd edn, New York and Oxford: Oxford University Press.

Hinds, S. (1998), *Allusion and Intertext: Dynamics of Appropriation in Roman Poetry*, Cambridge: Cambridge University Press.

Howarth, W. D. (1995), *Beaumarchais and the Theatre*, London and New York: Routledge.

Ireland, S. (2010), 'New Comedy', in G. Dobrov (ed.), *Brill's Companion to the Study of Greek Comedy*, 336–96, Leiden: Brill.

James, S. (2015), 'Mater, Oratio, Filia: Listening to Mothers in Roma Comedy', in D. Dutsch, S. James and D. Konstan (eds), *Women in Roman Republican Drama*, 108–27, Madison: University of Wisconsin Press.

Jocelyn, H. D. (1999), 'Code-switching in the *comoedia palliata*', in G. Vogt-Spira and B. Rommel (eds), *Rezeption und Identität: Die kulturelle Auseinandersetzung Roms mit Griechenland als europäisches Paradigma*, 169–95, Stuttgart: Franz Steiner Verlag.

Johnston, P. A. (1980), '*Poenulus* 1, 2 and Roman Women', *Transactions of the American Philological Association*, 110: 143–59.

Konstan, D. (2014), 'Turns and Returns in Plautus' *Casina*', in I. N. Perysinakis and E. Karakasis (eds), *Plautine Trends: Studies in Plautine Comedy and its Reception*, 3–11, Berlin: de Gruyter.

Kraus, A. N. (2004), 'Untaming the Shrew: Marriage, Morality and Plautine Comedy', PhD dissertation, Austin: University of Texas at Austin.

Lape, S. (2004), *Reproducing Athens: Menander's Comedy, Democratic Culture, and the Hellenistic City*, Princeton, NJ: Princeton University Press.

Leadbeater, L. W. (1986), '*Lubet* and the Principle of Pleasure in the Plays of Plautus', *Classical Bulletin*, 63: 5–11.

Leigh, M. (2000), 'Primitivism and Power: The Beginnings of Latin Literature', in O. Taplin (ed.), *Literature in the Greek and Roman Worlds: A New Perspective*, 288–301, Oxford: Oxford University Press.

Leigh, M. (2004), *Comedy and the Rise of Rome*, Oxford: Oxford University Press.

Leo, F. (1912), *Plautinische Forschungen*, Berlin: Weidmann Publishing.

Letessier, P. (2014), '*Quid istic est ornatus tuus?* Les surprises du costume dans les comédies de Plaute', in F. Gherchanoc and V. Huet (eds), *De la théâtralité du corps aux corps des dieux dans l'Antiquité*, 65–74, Brest: Centre de Recherche Bretonne et Celtique.

López López, M. (1991), *Los personajes de la Comedia plautina: nombre y función*, Lleida: Pagès editors.

Lowe, N.J. (2007), *Greece & Rome: New Surveys in the Classics 37: Comedy*, Cambridge: Cambridge University Press.

MacCary, W. T. (1973), 'The Significance of a Comic Pattern in Plautus and Beaumarchais', *Comparative Literature*, 88: 1262–87.

MacCary, W. T. (1975a), 'Patterns of Myth, Ritual, and Comedy in Plautus' *Casina*', *Texas Studies in Literature and Language*, 15: 881–9.

MacCary, W. T. (1975b), 'The Bacchae in Plautus' *Casina*', *Hermes*, 103: 459–63.

MacCary, W. T. and Willcock, M. M. (1976), *Plautus: Casina*, Cambridge: Cambridge University Press.

Maclennan, K. and Stockert, W. (2016), *Plautus: Aulularia*, Liverpool: Liverpool University Press.

Malamud, M. (2001), 'A Funny Thing Happened on the Way from Brooklyn: Roman Comedy on Broadway and in Film', *Arion*, 8: 33–51.

Manuwald, G. (2011), *Roman Republican Theatre: A History*, Cambridge: Cambridge University Press.

Marshall, C. W. (2006), *The Stagecraft and Performance of Roman Comedy*, Cambridge: Cambridge University Press.

Marshall, C. W. (2015), 'Domestic Sexual Labor in Plautus', *Helios*, 42: 123–41.

Mattingly, H. B. (1960), 'The First Period of Plautine Revival', *Latomus*, 19: 230–52.

McCarthy, K. (2000), *Slaves, Masters and the Art of Authority in Plautine Comedy*, Princeton, NJ: Princeton University Press.

McElduff, S. (2013), *Roman Theories of Translation: Surpassing the Source*, London: Routledge.

Miola, R. (1993), 'The *Merry Wives of Windsor*: Classical and Italian', *Comparative Drama*, 27: 364–76.

Moore, T. J. (1994), 'Seats and Social Status in the Plautine Theatre', *Classical Journal*, 90: 113–23.

Moore, T. J. (1998), *The Theater of Plautus: Playing to the Audience*, Austin: University of Texas Press.

Moore, T. J. (2012), *Music in Roman Comedy*, Cambridge: Cambridge University Press.

Most, G. W. (2003), 'Violets in Crucibles: Translating, Traducing, Transmuting', *Transactions of the American Philological Association*, 133: 381–90.

Nervegna, S. (2013), *Menander in Antiquity: The Contexts of Reception*, Cambridge: Cambridge University Press.

O'Bryhim, S. D. (1989), 'The Originality of Plautus' *Casina*', *American Journal of Philology*, 110: 81–103.

Ormand, K. (2009), *Controlling Desires: Sexuality in Ancient Greece and Rome*, Westport, CT: Praeger Publishing.

Panayotakis, C. (2005), 'Comedy, Atellane Farce and Mime', in S. Harrison, ed., *A Companion to Latin Literature*, 130–47, Malden, MA: Wiley-Blackwell.

Parker, H. N. (1997), 'The Teratogenic Grid', in J. P. Hallett and M. B. Skinner (eds), *Roman Sexualities*, 47–65, Princeton, NJ: Princeton University Press.

Parkin, T. G. (2003), *Old Age in the Roman World: A Cultural and Social History*, Baltimore, MD: Johns Hopkins University Press.

Petrides, A. (2014), 'Plautus between Greek Comedy and Atellan Farce: Assessments and Reassessments', in M. Fontaine and A. C. Scafuro (eds), *The Oxford Handbook of Greek and Roman Comedy*, 424–43, Oxford: Oxford University Press.

Petrone, G. (1983), *Teatro antico e inganno: Finzioni plautine*, Palermo: Palumbo.

Petrone, G. (2007), '... *Magis ... unicast ... pater*. Crisi dell'autorità senile', in T. Baier (ed.), *Generationenkonflikte auf der Bühne: Perspektiven im antiken und mittelalterlichen Drama*, 101–11, Tübingen: Narr.

Petrone, G. (2014), 'A letto con un caprone: Un topos comico (Plaut. *Cas.* 1018; Catull. 69 e 71)', *Bollettino di studi latini*, 44: 7–20.

Philippides, K. (2015), 'Plautus' *Casina*: The Punishment of *raphanidosis* and the Reversal of the Wife's Role', *Logeion*, 5: 242–59.

Questa, C. (2001), *Titus Maccius Plautus:* Casina, Urbino: QuattroVenti.

Rawson, B., ed. (1986), *The Family in Ancient Rome: New Perspectives*, Ithaca, NY: Cornell University Press.

Rei, A. (1998), 'Villains, Wives, and Slaves in the Comedies of Plautus', in S. R. Joshel and S. Murnaghan (eds), *Women and Slaves in Greco-Roman Culture: Differential Equations*, 98–108, London: Routledge.

Richlin, A. (2017), *Slave Theater in the Roman Republic: Plautus and Popular Comedy*, Cambridge: Cambridge University Press.

Rosenmeyer, P. A. (1995), 'Enacting the Law: Plautus' Use of the Divorce Formula on Stage', *Phoenix*, 49: 201–17.

Saller, R. P. (1994), *Patriarchy, Property and Death in the Roman Family*, Cambridge: Cambridge University Press.

Sbrocchi, L. G. and Campbell, J. D. (1992), *The Marescalco* (Il Marescalco), Carleton Renaissance Plays in Translation, Ottawa: Dovehouse Editions Canada.

Segal, E. (1987), *Roman Laughter: The Comedy of Plautus*, 2nd edn, New York and Oxford: Oxford University Press.

Sharrock, A. (1996), 'The Art of Deceit: *Pseudolus* and the Art of Reading', *Classical Quarterly*, 46: 152–74.

Sharrock, A. (2009), *Reading Roman Comedy: Poetics and Playfulness in Plautus and Terence*, Cambridge: Cambridge University Press.

Sices, D. and Atkinson, J. B. (1985), *The Comedies of Machiavelli*, Hanover, NH, and London: University Press of New England.

Skinner, M. (2005), *Sexuality in Greek and Roman Culture*, Malden, MA: Blackwell.

Slater, N. W. (1985), *Plautus in Performance: The Theatre of the Mind*, Princeton, NJ: Princeton University Press.

Slater, N. W. (1987), 'Transformations of Space in New Comedy', in J. Redmond (ed.), *Themes in Drama 9: The Theatrical Space*, 1–10, Cambridge: Cambridge University Press.

Spackman, B. (2010), 'Machiavelli and Gender', in J. M. Najemy (ed.), *The Cambridge Companion to Machiavelli*, 223–38, Cambridge: Cambridge University Press.

Stewart, R. (2012), *Plautus and Roman Slavery*, Malden, MA: Wiley-Blackwell.

Strong, A. K. (2016), *Prostitutes and Matrons in the Roman World*, Cambridge: Cambridge University Press.

Suárez, M. A. (2007), 'En torno al acto V de *Casina: flagitium, flagitatio* y perdón', *Myrtia*, 22: 95–104.

Tarrant, R. J. (1983), 'Plautus', in L. D. Reynolds (ed.), *Texts and Transmission*, 302–7, Oxford: Oxford University Press.

Tatum, J. (1983), *Plautus: The Darker Comedies*, Baltimore, MD: Johns Hopkins University Press.

Terpening, R. (1997), *Lodovico Dolce, Renaissance Man of Letters*, Toronto: University of Toronto Press.

Tobias, A. J. (1980), 'Bacchiac Women and Iambic Slaves in Plautus', *Classical World*, 73: 9–18.

Traill, A. (2011), '*Casina* and *The Comedy of Errors*', *International Journal of the Classical Tradition*, 18: 497–522.

Treggiari, S. (1991), *Roman Marriage*, Oxford: Oxford University Press.

Venuti, L. (2008), *The Translator's Invisibility: A History of Translation*, 2nd edn, London and New York: Routledge.

Watson, A. (1967), *The Law of Persons in the Later Roman Republic*, Oxford: Oxford University Press.

Way, M. L. (2000), 'Violence and Performance in Plautus' *Casina*', *Helios*, 27: 187–206.

Webster, T. B. L. (1970), *Studies in Later Greek Comedy*, 2nd edn, Manchester: Manchester University Press.

Weissinger, R. T. (1940), *A Study of Act Divisions in Classical Drama*, Scottdale, PA: Mennonite Publishing House.

Wiles, D. (1989), 'Marriage and Prostitution in Classical New Comedy', in J. Redmond (ed.), *Themes in Drama 11: Women in Theatre*, 31–48, Cambridge: Cambridge University Press.

Wiles, D. (1991), *The Masks of Menander: Sign and Meaning in Greek and Roman Performance*, Cambridge: Cambridge University Press.

Williams, B. (1993), 'Games People Play: Metatheatre as Performance Criticism in Plautus' *Casina*', *Ramus*, 22: 33–59.

Williams, C. A. (2010), *Roman Homosexuality*, 2nd edn, Oxford and New York: Oxford University Press.

Williams, G. (1958), 'Some Aspects of Roman Marriage Ceremonies and Ideals', *Journal of Roman Studies*, 48: 16–29.

Index